THIS MODERN MUSIC

THIS MODERN MUSIC

A GUIDE FOR THE
BEWILDERED LISTENER

John Tasker Howard

Essay Index Reprint Series

BOOKS FOR LIBRARIES PRESS
FREEPORT, NEW YORK

STANDARD BOOK NUMBER:
8369-0018-9

LIBRARY OF CONGRESS CATALOG CARD NUMBER:
68-58796

PRINTED IN THE UNITED STATES OF AMERICA

TO

Ernest LaPrade

TABLE OF CONTENTS

THIS MODERN MUSIC

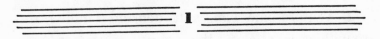

PEOPLE HAVE NEVER LIKED

MODERN MUSIC—AT FIRST

IT IS NOT at all strange that people generally do not like modern music, particularly those of us who have arrived at middle age. Our ancestors didn't like it either, even though their modern music was written by Monteverdi, Mozart, Beethoven, and Wagner. Civilized human beings are by nature too complacent to like violent changes, and older generations have always lamented the passing of "the good old days." Even the most adventurous pioneers take with them as much of their home environment as they can carry, and as soon as they have made a permanent settlement, they recreate as much of the atmosphere of their former homes as the geography and climate of their new surroundings will permit. Thus, we find New England architecture in Ohio, Spanish buildings in California, and Chinatowns in our large cities.

If venturesome emigrants demand familiar surroundings, what about those of us who stay at home,
among the same neighbors, working at the same jobs,
playing the same old games? Fashion designers may
create radical changes from season to season to force
people to buy new clothes, but most husbands resent
the way their wives look in their new hats as much
as they are annoyed by the bills. And if anything so
trivial as a new set of contract bridge conventions is
upsetting to our peace of mind, is it any wonder that
the New Deal gave everyone the jitters?

Most of us admit, however, that the world is changing: socially, economically, and politically, so whether
we like it or not, we know that our mode of life will
have to be adapted to the world about us. Yet, while
we are broadminded and practical enough to accomplish this growth in the major matters of life, it seems
to some of us a bit futile and unnecessary to disturb
ourselves with changes in the less vital things, among
them, music.

Music, however, is a living language; or rather, *good*
music is. It is composed by human beings, and human
beings do have to adapt themselves to shifting conditions, no matter how much they resist them at first.
Hence, if music is to remain a living language, that is,
if it is to be a sincere and honest expression of the

(2)

men and women who compose it, it too must grow. Like all languages, it must constantly acquire new words and expressions to convey its meaning in a changing society.

The same principle is true of any language. Greek and Latin are dead languages because they are not used any more for daily conversation; they belonged to past civilizations and have not been adapted to more recent affairs. There are no Greek and Latin words for oil-burner, cocktail, movies, or broadcasting. The dictionaries and grammars of living languages —modern Greek and Italian, English, French, German—are continually revised and brought up-to-date by the inclusion of new words, and of new phrases and sentence constructions formerly considered bad usage.

It is because music is a living language that we have the so-called modern music. Music is a medium that is constantly increasing its vocabulary and taking into its grammar various devices of harmony, melody and rhythm that were formerly forbidden by rule. If it failed to accomplish such changes it would soon be as dead as Greek and Latin, and interesting chiefly to historians.

The term "modern," as applied to music, is so vague in its meaning that it will be well to clarify it and agree on its definition. Since the general conception of "mod-

ern music" is that of something which sounds strange
and startling, the phrase has become elastic and relative, depending on the experience and taste of the
individual who listens to it. To some, Debussy is still
a modernist, even though a number of his works are
in the standard repertory of concert artists and conservative music teachers. To others, Stravinsky's *Fire
Bird* and even his *Rite of Spring* are no longer modern,
but have become altogether "old hat." Thus, the significance of the term depends on the point of view of
the individual listener, on whether he has become accustomed to more recent idioms or whether he has
exposed himself so infrequently to the works of the
last half-century that he still holds the composers of
Beethoven's day as the norm and standard of all music,
past and present.

Ernst Křenek, in *Music Here and Now*,[1] distin-
guishes between three kinds of present-day music:
contemporary, modern, and new. He maintains that
"contemporary" music consists of whatever is composed by contemporaries of the person using the term.
Thus, anything written by a living composer is contemporary, regardless of its content or style. "Modern"
music does not depend solely on the date of composition, but is that part of contemporary music which

[1] New York: W. W. Norton & Company, Inc., 1939.

deviates from tradition in its material and in its style. The third group, "new" music, is the type which, "because of its essential qualities, experiences the greatest opposition to its conversion into merchandise"; in other words, that which encounters the greatest resistance from the general public, and from program-makers and commercial publishers.

Obviously, this volume will consider as modern such music as falls in Křenek's second and third groups: that which is different from the traditional styles of past centuries, and which finds general acceptance difficult. We need not be concerned with music that is old-fashioned and conventional in style, even though it was composed as recently as last month. And since the term is entirely relative, we shall have to consider the modern music of various periods and places. In other words, Mozart wrote modern music in the latter eighteenth century, so we are concerned with Mozart's music. John Smith, in the year 1942, writes music that Mozart might have written, so we shall not bother our heads with it.

It may be that the music of our day is far more radical, and breaks more sharply with tradition, than did the new music of Mozart, Beethoven, or Mendelssohn, though the conservative music-lovers of those days thought their new music shocking enough. Go back even further, to the sixteenth century, and you find Claudio Monteverdi causing as much furor by championing the major-minor tonal system as Schoenberg has caused in our time with his atonality. In the year 1600 a critic wrote of Monteverdi: "Though I am glad of a new manner of composition, it would be more edifying to find in these madrigals reasonable passages, but these kinds of air-castles and chimeras deserve the severest reproof. . . . You hear a medley of sounds, a variety of parts that are intolerable to the ear. . . . With all the best will in the world, how can the mind see light in this chaos?"

Not many of us today would think of Mozart as a disconcerting modernist, but read what an eighteenth-century critic thought of his latest string quartets: "It is a pity that in his truly artistic and beautiful compositions Mozart should carry his effort after originality too far, to the detriment of the sentiment and heart of his works. His new quartets . . . are much too highly spiced to be palatable for any length of time."

A Vienna music patron had several of these quartets performed at his home, and was so enraged at finding the dissonances in one of them actually printed in the music that he tore the parts to pieces. Haydn, however, remarked that if Mozart wrote his music with

dissonances, he must have had good reasons for doing so.

Beethoven was a shocking radical. He opened his
C major symphony, the first, with a chord from the
key of F, and passed through the key of G before
getting down to business in C, the ruling key of
the symphony. At one point in his third symphony, the
Eroica, he had two different chords sounded at the
same time. A contemporary critic explained this by
saying that "poor Beethoven is so deaf that he cannot hear the discords he writes." One conductor went
so far as to correct the "error" at rehearsal.

The composers of the romantic movement—Chopin,
Mendelssohn, Schubert, Schumann, Brahms, Wagner
—were all resisted by the conservatives and reaction-
aries of their time. Robert Schumann's teacher never
forgave him for admiring Chopin, and when Schumann
championed the young Brahms, he was a lone prophet
crying in a classic wilderness.

Music is almost always an expression of the age in
which it is written. If it isn't, we may be sure that the
composer himself belongs spiritually to another age,
or that he patterns his work after the music of earlier
composers, unconsciously or perhaps deliberately.
Then we say that his style is Wagnerian, or Franckian,
instead of John Smithian.

(7)

This does not mean that originality alone is a sign of greatness, or even a virtue in itself. Progress and change are by no means synonymous. Many things may be wholly original and yet be altogether worthless, and it must be admitted that some composers sacrifice a great deal for what they believe to be originality. It seems as though their chief concern is to keep their music from bearing even the slightest resemblance to anything that has been written before. In such cases, the composer is substituting for sincere expression a conscious style which will inevitably prove artificial and manufactured. If he announces that he never listens to other men's works for fear it will destroy his individuality, he is explaining the limitations of his own music.

The casual listener to music, in the concert hall or on the radio and phonograph, may wonder how he can possibly distinguish between the genuine article and the work of a charlatan. How, for example, is the man to whom the connecting links of a Beethoven symphony are still a mystery, to know whether Stravinsky's *Rite of Spring* is an authentic art expression, which he ought to like, or merely a confusion of shocking, ugly sounds? And how is he to acquire the ability to enjoy anything which is at first hearing so highly unpleasant to his ears and his nervous system? Why torture himself by listening to it?

These are the questions this book will try to answer. The music lover must make up his mind that he is going to hear a great deal of modern music if he goes to concerts, or listens to all the numbers on a radio program. If he buys tickets to hear a Beethoven symphony, he may have to listen first to a ballet-suite by Stravinsky. Even if he is willing to come late and miss half of what he is paying for, his wife, or whomever he is taking to the concert, may like Stravinsky, and insist that they hear the entire program.

He needn't feel too badly if he thinks the whole business a terrible mess. If the new music is being played for the first time, he will no doubt have plenty of company in his opinion among the professional critics. And he has a distinct advantage over the critics; he may express his opinions to any or all of his friends, and suffer no ill consequences. He has little to lose if the ensuing years prove him wrong. The critic, however, must go on record in print, and allow historians of the future to dig in the files and show him up to posterity.

And how often these unfortunate gentlemen have turned out to be wrong, down through the history of music right to the present day! Gounod once remarked that César Franck's D minor symphony represented the height of incompetence carried to dogmatic lengths, while the late Richard Aldrich described Rimsky-Korsakoff's *Scheherazade* as "dull," with an "insistence on long drawn oriental chantings and dronings." [2]

The following paragraph might well describe the worthless product of a third- or fourth-rate composition student:

"Last night's concert began with a lot of impressionistic daubs of color smeared higgledy-piggledy on a tonal palette, with never a thought of form or purpose except to create new combinations of sounds. . . . One thing only was certain, and that was that the composer's ocean was a frog-pond, and that some of its denizens had got into the throat of every one of the brass instruments."

Those words were written for the New York *Tribune* of March 22, 1907, by Henry E. Krehbiel, one of the soundest and most learned critics who has ever written for a metropolitan journal, and the work he described was Debussy's *La Mer*. Fifteen years later Krehbiel again reviewed a performance of *La Mer*, and called it a "poetic work in which Debussy has so wondrously caught the rhythms and colors of the seas."

The inference to be drawn from these two opinions is clear. When Krehbiel first heard *La Mer,* its strangeness confused him. Fifteen years later he had absorbed the idiom, and become so familiar with it that it had ceased to bother him, and he was able to grasp the true beauty of the work.

Read also what Krehbiel wrote about the Fourth Symphony of Tschaikowsky when he first heard it, in 1890: [8]

"Of the four symphonies of Tschaikowsky which have been heard in New York, it is far and away the least interesting. It is the first of the larger works of the genial Russian, concerning which we feel tempted to say that it ought not to have been performed at all. It would have been treated with manifest kindness if its *Scherzo* had been incorporated in the scheme of some popular concert and the rest of it had been consigned to the limbo of oblivion. The *Scherzo* utilizes the strings *pizzicato* throughout and is pretty. Artistically, it stands on the plane, say, of Strauss's *Pizzicato Polka,* though not quite as graceful. As a symphonic movement, it is about as dignified as one of the com-

[8] New York *Tribune,* Feb. 2, 1890.

positions which delight the souls of college banjo clubs. But in spite of the striving evidenced by Tschaikowsky's recurrence in his last movement to material used in the *Introduction* and the first movement . . . the composition can scarcely be called a *Symphony,* except on the principle of *lucus a non lucendo.* It wants nearly every element which makes the work which opened the concert, for instance [Mozart's G minor], a symphony. There was a great show of effort in the composition, but only a modicum of artistic result."

Again, the critic resisted something new. The first three symphonies of Tschaikowsky were conventional and, incidentally, are rarely if ever heard today. In the Fourth, Tschaikowsky ventured in new fields. He extended the traditional forms, and used a Russian folksong as a motto which tied the work together by recurring in the last movement. Krehbiel didn't like it; its novelty was so offensive to him that he missed entirely the power and dramatic force which have come to thrill thousands, perhaps millions, of music lovers.

Resistance to new music has always existed to a certain degree, particularly on the part of critics, but it is only in the last century and a half that it has become a violent and hostile public reaction. It was in the nineteenth century that the worship of the "old masters" came into being, with its establishment of a standard repertory for symphony orchestras and for individual concert-artists. Nowadays new music is played by major organizations largely for general prestige, as a contribution to the advancement of music, not as an immediate box-office attraction. Concert artists look for cash customers for Beethoven, Wagner, or Tschaikowsky; not for Joe Smith, nor even for Hindemith.

In the seventeen hundreds the situation was considerably different. The repertory had not yet come into existence, and new works were performed more often than old ones. Some of this may be explained by the fact that music was still largely the diversion of kings and princes, who maintained their own musicians to perform for the court. It was the duty of the *Kapellmeister* to engage and train the musicians of the court. Music to play was needed, of course, and generally the *Kapellmeister*, in his own handwriting, would arrange and adapt the parts for performance as an incidental part of his duties. He was expected to compose music of his own for all occasions, and even when he played other men's music, it was generally new. Thus, Prince Esterházy required Haydn to keep his private orchestra supplied with new symphonies, and his quartet with new chamber music.

At the Thomaskirche in Leipzig, Bach was expected to write a new cantata each week, and his large family was kept busy copying out the parts as the father finished each page of the score. During the several years that Bach was *Kapellmeister* for Prince Leopold at Köthen, he wrote the bulk of his orchestral and chamber music. But this was for performance by the Prince's musicians, not for publication. It was not until years later that these works were published and available for performance elsewhere.

When concerts for the public became regular features of European cities, particularly in England, the people apparently wanted new music at first, for the eighteenth-century newspaper announcements invariably featured new works. When Haydn went to London, the contract called for twelve new symphonies to be played at his concerts—six on each visit. There was also a demand from the British public for a constant supply of new operas, oratorios and instrumental works by Handel. In 1742 the Dublin papers announced that "on Monday, the 12th of April, for the benefit of the Prisoners of the several Gaols, and the support of Mercer's Hospital, In Stephen's-street, and of the Charitable Infirmary on the Inn's Quay, will be performed at the Musick Hall in Fishambe-street, Mr. Handel's *new Grand Oratorio, called the Messiah,* in which the Gentlemen of the Choirs of both Cathedrals will assist, with some Concertos on the Organ, by Mr. Handell."

It was the same in America. When George Washington visited Boston, a few months after his inauguration as president, a huge concert was planned in his honor. The newspapers announced that the program would contain the "Oratorio of *Jonah,* which has been applauded by the best judges and has never been performed in America." Again in Boston, a Mr. Turner advertised a concert in 1773, and respectfully begged leave "to acquaint his subscribers that his last concert for the season will be on Tues. eve, at which time will be performed a variety of music received from London by Capt. Scott, which never has been performed in this place."

All of this was in the eighteenth century. In the nineteenth century, concerts and opera became the diversion of the people, not alone the luxury of aristocrats. With the public demand for the familiar, there came a resistance to new music which made it difficult for young revolutionary composers to gain a sympathetic hearing. As Křenek has written: [4] "Theaters and concert halls were thrown open to an enormously increasing number of people, and the operation of

[4] *Music Here and Now: op. cit.*

music as an institution had thenceforth to depend for its sustenance upon this new audience's desire to buy and its power to buy, a service which formerly was essentially performed by small privileged groups." Thus, in our own time, we find that radical new music generally has its first hearing at non-profit-making concerts sponsored by groups of composers or subsidized by philanthropists.

The inexperienced layman, then, is not alone in his disinclination to bother himself with listening to modern music. Sometimes, however, he is more receptive to it than professionals are, for though he may like best the things he is familiar with, he is often far less hemmed-in by traditions than is the veteran concert-goer. Virgil Thomson has gone so far as to claim that modern music is easier for the layman to understand than old music. In an article on "Understanding Modern Music" he writes: [5]

"There is no reason why anybody in the music world, professional or layman, should find himself in the position of not understanding a piece of twentieth-century music, if he is willing to give himself a little trouble. . . . The art-music of the past, most of all that eighteenth and nineteenth century repertory known as 'clas-

[5] New York *Herald Tribune*, Jan. 4, 1942.

sical' music, is, on the other hand, about as incomprehensible as anything could be. Its idiom is comprehensible, because it is familiar. But its significant content is as impenetrable as that of the art work of the Middle Ages. It was made by men whose modes of thought and attitudes of passion were as different from ours as those of Voltaire and Goethe and Rousseau . . . were different from those of Bernard Shaw . . . and Gertrude Stein and Mickey Mouse. . . ."

It is surely too much to say that a twentieth-century listener cannot penetrate to the spiritual content of Beethoven, but Mr. Thomson is sound in stating that, aside from the idiom of a contemporary work, no listener can fail to penetrate its meaning, at least partially.

The listener's problem is one of understanding something of the composer's method, and of how his style differs from that of composers in the past. Then he can decide for himself whether or not the twentieth-century message is coherently and effectively expressed; in other words, he will know whether or not he is likely to enjoy a new composition when he has become used to its style and mode of expression.

If he is a lover of the classics, if he likes to listen to his "old favorites," he must realize why music must change its style with the centuries. In the next chapter we shall find how music expresses and reflects the background of the age in which it was composed. Thus, in the twentieth century, when a composer writes descriptive music, he will deal with the sights and sounds that belong to his own era, and instead of painting tone-pictures of sailing vessels he will depict the speedier locomotives and airplanes; instead of blacksmith shops, he will paint steel mills. In drawing his musical scenes, he finds that the melodic, rhythmic, and harmonic vocabulary of Beethoven will not suffice for the mighty roar of the plunging giant of steel, and like Honegger in *Pacific 231*, he will draw on new combinations of sounds to sing the song of the great locomotive. Nor will the chastely simple pattern of Handel's *Harmonious Blacksmith* serve for describing an iron foundry. The crude dissonances of Mossolow's *Soviet Iron Foundry* are less tuneful, but more faithful to their subject.

Entirely apart from the descriptive functions of music, how can we expect the musical speech of Handel to express the restless, uncertain temper of our age any more effectively than the literary style of *Godey's Lady's Book* would describe an air raid in the pages of *Life* or *Time*? The march of science, the invention of machines, have created an atmosphere wholly unlike the environment that surrounded our fathers.

We need music which expresses the way we feel in the year 1942, or in any current year in which we live. It is not sound to say that we have enough music already, for there must be music to express the voice of every age. If the music lovers of Mozart's day had refused altogether to listen to new music, we wouldn't have any Beethoven. And if the concert-goers of Beethoven's day had decided that they had enough music (which some of them almost did), then there would have been no Schumann, Mendelssohn, Wagner, or Brahms.

For unless we listen to our new music, it will not exist. When music is not performed, it is merely a set of symbols on paper. None of us can tell who the Mozarts or the Beethovens of the future will be, but we must make sure that when they come, if they are not here already, they'll have a chance to be heard.

There are just two things that the music-lover who wants to enjoy modern music need do. First, he must realize *why* it is what it is; why the composers of every age have written differently from those who preceded them. Secondly, he must acquaint himself, if only superficially, with a few of the methods used by modern composers to make their music different from eighteenth- and nineteenth-century music. Then he will know whether they have used their tools and materials effectively or inefficiently. And he may come to have a fair idea as to which of them are creative artists and which are mountebanks and fakers.

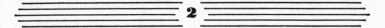

MUSIC TELLS HOW PEOPLE THINK,

AND ACT

PLATO ONCE wrote that the introduction of a new kind of music must be shunned as imperilling the whole state, since styles of music are never disturbed without affecting the most important institutions. "The new style," he explained, "quietly insinuates itself into manners and customs, and from these it issues a greater force . . . goes on to attack laws and constitutions, displaying the utmost impudence, until it ends by overturning everything, both in public and in private."

If this were true, it might be urged that jazz and swing are responsible for most of the world's troubles in the twentieth century. It would indeed be novel to argue that our social and political systems have been moulded by the music which people of every age have played and sung. But even though Plato's theory is too extreme to be plausible, we do know that the reverse is true; that the music of each period in history is a reflection of the life, the temperament, and the viewpoints of that era.

It is generally recognized that the songs people sing, particularly the so-called popular songs, provide a year-by-year record of the lives of those people. Superficially, these songs and ballads record happenings of importance, the names and deeds of popular heroes, fashions in dress, slang phrases and colloquialisms, sports and games, occupations and professions, means of transportation, almost everything connected with every-day life. Beneath the surface, however, is even more important information; revelation of states of minds and points of view. Such a record is found not only in the words of songs, but in the spirit of the music itself, in its very style and idiom. If we bear in mind the character and surroundings of the people for whom the music of each age was written, we shall understand their music more clearly. Conversely, the student of history will do well to become familiar with the representative music of the age he is studying. It provides a vivid description of the background that produced historical events, and explains why people acted as they did. Honest music, that which is sincere, is invariably an expression of the era which produced it.

Take, for example, the merry lilt of the English madrigals from the sixteenth century. These songs embody the underlying spirit of Merrie England in the days of Queen Elizabeth, when Britain was growing rich and enjoying the things which come with economic prosperity. There was joy in life, and people sang and danced to the jolly strains of music by Byrd and Gibbons.

Moving on a century, to Continental Europe, we approach an era when outer forms become more important than inner thoughts. Instead of being the unrestrained voicing of joy or sorrow, emotional expressions are more polished. Tenderness, rather than passion, marks the art of the day, and beauty is fragile and delicate. The placid beauty of Gluck's melodies are characterized by restraint and chaste refinement.

Johann Sebastian Bach lived in an age (1685–1750) when men did not wear their hearts on their coatsleeves. Thus, superficially, Bach seems to be preoccupied with form and structure, and the emotional depths of his works, almost unfathomable, are apparent only to those who are familiar with them. It was undoubtedly the early eighteenth-century insistence on form that lent this aspect to Bach's music.

This was also an age when the princely rulers of Europe showed their power through costly and elaborate architecture, and we find the composers of the day, Bach included, showing an intense devotion to detail, decorating their music with delicate instrumental patterns which were continually repeated and imitated contrapuntally.

In the eighteenth century, concert music was not for the people, but for the nobility. In the preceding chapter we found that concerts were mostly given in the palaces of kings and princes, not in public concert-halls. The musician was not a man of social rank; he generally ate his meals in the servants' hall. Consequently we find a lowly and humble spirit whenever a musician addressed his patron. Today the great Bach has a seat with the immortals, but read the words he addressed to the Margrave of Brandenburg, who is known to us only because he commissioned six concerti from Johann Sebastian Bach. In his letter the composer begged the Margrave not to judge the imperfections of the concerti "by the severity of the fine and delicate taste that every one knows You to have for music, but rather to consider benignly the profound respect and the very humble obedience to which they are meant to testify."

It was naturally the taste of the princely patrons of

music which determined the style of music written by composers dependent on these aristocrats for support. And the music, in turn, gives us an intimate picture of the life at their courts. It was a day when art, religion, letters, were highly organized and designed chiefly for the glory of absolute monarchs. The luxurious court at Versailles was the model for every king, prince and courtier of Europe. Manners were polished and stilted, and conversations were witty and marked by a cynicism that often became malicious. Although the music of Haydn and Mozart is filled with grace and tenderness, and exaltation, too, it is nevertheless highly formalized, dealing with the artificialities rather than the realities of life. The dance forms these composers used—the minuet, the gavotte—picture powdered wigs and knee breeches with silver buckles, rather than the rollicking, boisterous good times of Beethoven's peasant-folk. Even when Haydn used Croatian folk-songs, he polished them so that they would be fit for the salons of Counts and Barons. If any indication were needed to show the great genius of these composers, it is the fact that their music is spontaneous and vital in spite of the formal restrictions imposed upon it.

It is often said that Beethoven was the link between the so-called classic and romantic periods of music. It is quite true that his early style was a definite reflection of his predecessors, particularly of Mozart, while his mature works represent a break with tradition that ushered in the freedom from convention of the eighteenth century romanticists. Compare Beethoven's country dances with any of Haydn's minuets and you will see how one was writing of peasants and villagers where the other wrote of kings and princes.

In music Beethoven was a revolutionary; for his time, almost a radical. That was because he lived in an age of revolutions, when the elegant, cynical courts of Europe were tottering. In 1783 the American colonists won their fight for freedom, and less than ten years later the French Revolution cost Louis the Sixteenth and the beautiful Marie Antoinette their heads as well as their crowns. All of this gave courage to writers and artists who strove for freedom in expressing their ideas.

Beethoven was a revolutionary in thought, as well as in his music. He caught the spirit of the French revolt, and when Napoleon appeared as an ardent champion of freedom, a leader who would restore order and prosperity to his people, Beethoven put him on a pedestal and resolved to write a symphony in his honor. He began the work in 1803, and by 1804 the first draft was ready. It lay on his desk where all who came to see him could read the name "Bonaparte" inscribed on the title-page. Then came the news that Napoleon had assumed the title of Emperor, and the disillusioned Beethoven ripped the title-page from his music. But the symphony remained the *Eroica,* the portrait of a hero, a champion of the people, even though Napoleon had ceased to be that hero.

It was such music which prepared the way for the romantic era, when the actual content of music, what it had to say, became more important than the form in which it said it. Before the romanticists, music had seemed to be principally concerned with the classic forms—the sonata, the rondo, the classic dance-forms, and others; it was afraid to let itself go and to abandon itself to its mood. With the nineteenth century, and the revolts of the common people which led eventually to the Central Europe uprisings of 1848, artists, musicians and writers felt free to indulge their fancies. Just as the political thought of the day insisted upon more freedom for the individual, so did art, literature and music become a more personal expression of the artist's own view of life, rather than that of his patron.

The old forms in music were by no means abandoned; composers still wrote symphonies in the traditional sonata-form, but the forms became more elastic, and were adapted to the individual ideas the composers wished to express. Harmonic combinations became richer and more varied, and musicians had the courage to make a freer use of the dissonances we shall discuss in the next chapter.

A closer relationship developed between music and poetry, and poetic ideas. Robert Schumann gave fanciful, descriptive titles to dozens of his piano pieces, and even when he wrote absolute, non-descriptive, music in traditional forms, it was always the personal expression of his poetic nature. The slow movements—from his symphonies, his Piano Quintet, his Piano Concerto —are far more intense and foreboding than the works which come from an earlier century.

Chopin filled his works with sorrow for the tribulations of his native Poland and he also achieved freedom from many of the shackles of musical convention. He advanced the development of free forms—the fantasy, the impromptu, the ballade—which are forms determined by the musical material itself.

The lovely melodies of Franz Schubert were aimed directly at the hearts of the people around him; they were not designed for lords and ladies in silks and satins. Schubert reflected the time in which he lived, as well as his own lovable nature.

Like Beethoven, Richard Wagner was a free-thinker in his philosophy, as well as in his music. During the

Revolutions of 1848 his political ideas became so widely known that he was forced to flee to Zurich and live in exile for nearly twelve years. In some of his music-dramas he embodied his social and political ideas. The *Ring of the Nibelungs* was a protest against forces which Wagner considered evil. And in regard to the music itself, it was the background of the age he lived in that made Wagner dissatisfied with the restrictions which had enslaved the music of an earlier day. He used his great genius to free music from its shackles.

That is the spirit we feel when we listen to the overpowering masterpieces Wagner left us—the upward reaching of a great soul (and he was that in spite of his selfishness and disloyalty to his friends) who longed to be rid of the pettiness of earthly things; a surging that had no patience with formality or even politeness. As we look at history, we realize that this music could not possibly have been composed in the days of Bach, of Haydn, nor of Mozart.

The rise of nationalism in music was another movement which had its origin in nineteenth-century history. Just as the coming of democracy dethroned kings and gave to the peoples a new consciousness of their rights and privileges, so also, with the old barriers swept away, and with small duchies overthrown, there came the idea that people speaking the same language and sharing the same customs should be politically united as nations. Thus the political upheavals ushered in not only the romantic era in the arts, but also a feeling for nationalism. Mikhail Glinka, in Russia, was one of the first to express this spirit, and his opera, *Russlan and Ludmilla,* is generally regarded as the foundation of a distinctively Russian music. Its themes were based largely on Russian folk-songs Glinka had heard in his youth, and some of the music was so true to the life of the lower classes of society that a group of noblemen sneeringly called it "the music of coachmen." Following Glinka were other composers of the Russian nationalist school: Borodin, Moussorgsky, Balakirev, Glazounow, Rimsky-Korsakoff.

As states became composed of citizens, rather than subjects, the ideas and emotions of nationality were free to develop. The type of thought which shaped institutions and governments also affected the music of those peoples and races which were the most nationalistic in spirit. Czecho-Slovakia, a nation whose political freedom was denied for several centuries, was typical of this movement. As far back as 1620 the Czechs and the Slovaks were brought under the rule of the Austrian Hapsburgs. They were forbidden to speak their own language, and their rulers sought to stamp out all traces of the Czech national spirit. Beneath the surface, however, the national feeling was kept alive, and was probably made more vital by the very oppression which sought to destroy it. In 1859 the restrictions were somewhat relaxed, and Bohemian artists came forward who were filled with the national spirit of their countrymen. The leading composer to express this spirit was Friedrich Smetana, and his opera, *The Bartered Bride,* contains many of the songs and dances of his homeland. After Smetana came Antonin Dvořák, whose *Slavonic Dances* vividly express the color and life of his countrymen.

Jan Sibelius (1865———) is one of the most nationalistic of composers, and is universally recognized as the musical voice of Finland. Since he is still living, and because his works are among the most performed of those by present-day composers, he is often looked upon as a modern composer. It is true that his music is contemporary in time, but in spirit he is actually a romanticist, heroic and epic, expressing with rare eloquence the aspirations of his fellow-countrymen. His idiom is unmistakably his own, but it does not enter twentieth-century experimental fields. His first symphony derived almost directly from Tschaikowsky. In the second symphony, composed in 1901, he managed to cast aside the reminders of Tschaikowsky, and wrote a work which the Finns accepted as an expression of their revolt against oppression. Its climaxes rise to exultant heights. The earlier tone-poem, *Finlandia,* composed in 1894, expressed so fervently the national spirit of the Finns, that its performance was at one time forbidden by the Russian government.

Sibelius's seven symphonies, as well as his tone-poems and the violin concerto, represent a progressive series of steps in the composer's development. He has devised his own structures and evolved his own melodic harmonic style, neither startling nor revolutionary, but altogether typical of Sibelius and of Finland.

In Spain, Italy, Norway, and the British Isles, the music of nationalist composers has pictured the temperament of the peoples, their customs and ways of life, their folk-lore and legends, and the very climates in which they live. The songs and instrumental pieces of Edvard Grieg bring to us the icy blasts of the Northland as vividly as Neapolitan folk-songs breathe the warm sunshine of southern Italy.

National consciousness in America awakened slowly. We have been such a cosmopolitan nation, composed of so many races of Europe, that our nationalism cannot take the form of a unified racial expression, but must be a spirit which comes from a welding of all the elements which make up our population. True

Americanism in art, music and literature, must be based on our ideals, our aspirations, our institutions, and our philosophy. In the twentieth century, when we have become independent in thought, just as we became independent in action a century before, our national spirit is asserting itself, and our composers are writing music which is not a mere reflection of European music, but which actually springs from the cities, the factories, and the countryside of America.

One of our leading composers, Howard Hanson, has expressed some pertinent ideas about nationalism in American music. Hanson was born in Wahoo, Nebraska, in 1896, of a Swedish descent which finds expression in his first symphony, the *Nordic*. He believes that every race must write its own music, and that truly American music must come out of the life of America. To him American music is simply music written by Americans, and it does not matter whether the composers are descendants of New England or Virginia settlers, or whether they are the sons or daughters of recently arrived immigrants.

Hanson's long list of works includes three symphonies, of which the second (*Romantic*) and the third are frequently performed. His opera, *Merrymount*, was produced at the Metropolitan, New York, in 1934. In addition to composing, he is Director of the Eastman School of Music at Rochester, New York, and as conductor of the American Composers' Concerts at Rochester he has introduced many works by his colleagues.

While Hanson is not an advocate of anything that might be termed an American "school" in music, he does believe that American music has acquired nationalistic traits, in the definite personalities of many of our younger composers, and in the spiritual individuality of their works.

Thus we find that all movements and changes—political, social, economic—which have affected the direction and course of human life, have shaped the character of the music of various ages, just as they have affected literature and the other arts. After romanticism, came post-romanticism, somewhat decadent, and often filled with the neuroticism of a Tschaikowsky. This was an era of general decadence, when new changes were on the horizon, but when established customs were still so firmly intrenched that to question them was to place oneself apart from convention. The conventions and the traditions had grown soft, however, and lacked the rugged vitality of an earlier century, when they themselves had been revolutionary, and had replaced those of a still earlier day.

And so we come to our own time, when our music

is showing such startling changes, such radical departures from older music, that it seems to the traditionalist to be nothing but inexcusable noise. But once again we have merely to consider the events of our own time to find the reason. Even before the first World War, life had become more complex than it had ever been before. The changes that have occurred so rapidly and so suddenly would have required centuries in the middle ages. Science and invention have made such rapid strides in the last quarter-century that civilization will require several generations to catch up with them, and to learn how to use their products intelligently. Where the first World War seemed to be a liberation of oppressed peoples— Czecho-Slovakia, Poland, Finland—the second World War has for a time overthrown all that. Peoples who had been held in subjection a century before are again enslaved. Their nationalism is suppressed, and they may express openly only what their conquerors allow them to say. The art of the totalitarian states is controlled by those who govern them; composers may write only such music as embodies the ideology of political dictatorships.

In America we are still free to voice our feelings, and so are those composers from Europe who have fled to our shores. America has become the cradle of an art which will tell the future historian how people felt and acted in these troubled times.

Our modern music tells of the feverish pace at which we are living. When we dance, we have not the patience for the slow steps of the minuet, or the smooth, gliding motions of the waltz; we spend our energies on the rhumba and the conga; or else we jitterbug. Life is so much more complex that our young people are as sophisticated as their grandfathers, and as wise, if not wiser, to the affairs of the world. So our music is complex and sophisticated, and much of it, particularly our popular music, appeals chiefly to the younger generation.

It is, perhaps, the noisiness and confusion of our modern music which disturb us most. But they, too, are a direct reflection of modern life. Carl Engel wrote of this almost fifteen years ago, in an article entitled "Harking Back and Looking Forward":[1]

"What we need most of all is an explanation for the probable connection between the latest changes in music and the increase in noise. The progress of music is based on and conditioned by the necessity of constantly overcoming fatigue. And the fatigue of the ear has been hastened or aggravated by the alarming in-

[1] *Musical Quarterly,* Jan., 1928.

crease in noise to which modern life is subjecting us. Probably our whole nervous system is affected by it, and not to its profit. Where two hundred years ago melodious street-calls announced the approach of itinerant vendors and the song of an ungreased axle-tree merely emphasized the ordinary stillness, we have now the involved and strident counterpoint of traffic over an ostinato of policemen's whistles and automobile horns. The timid tinkle of the spinet has been replaced by the aggressive tones of the 'loud speaker.' Loudness and coarseness go hand in hand. Pandemonium in the street, and the home a jazz dive or a roaring Chautauqua—truly the art of music is hard put to devise new stimuli wherewith to counteract the growing aural disturbance. The wonderful and consoling fact is that music, apparently, is equal to any occasion."

Strangely enough, our young people are bothered not at all by the discords of their swing music; nor by the dissonance of modern concert music. They have been brought up on it, and have not been compelled to switch their ears from the leisurely syncopation of old-fashioned ragtime to the frenetic chaos of recent times. Perhaps, then, it is because older ears are tuned to the nineteenth century that they are constantly comparing our new music with that of their youth. If they had never heard Beethoven or Mozart, Schoenberg and Stravinsky might not sound strange at all. Certainly traditional Hindu music seems perfectly natural to the Hindus, yet to us its scales are strange and new, and its rhythms almost incomprehensible.

We may well wonder what the music of the future will be; where it can go that it has not already gone. Perhaps there will be a reaction from the radical experiments of the past quarter-century; there are distinct signs that it has already begun. But whatever course the development of modern music takes, of one thing we may be certain: it will definitely reflect its background, and the ultimate fate of civilization will be vividly recorded in the music that is composed during the coming years. Aspirations, ideals, as well as frustrations, will prove the determining factors in shaping this art-expression, and the various devices and patterns of atonality, polytonality, and others which we shall discuss in succeeding chapters, will be only the means by which the composer will convey his inner thoughts to his audience.

THIS MODERN MUSIC

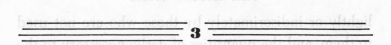

3

DISSONANCE—THE SALT AND PEPPER

OF MUSIC

IF IT WERE not for dissonance, music would be an altogether insipid affair. Listening to it would prove monotonous and cloying, just like reading a novel in which all the characters are annoyingly good, and everything connected with the plot is Utopian. The pleasant things of life are pleasant in contrast to the unpleasant, and it's because bad things exist that we enjoy the good ones.

Food without salt is unexciting and tasteless, and some dishes require a liberal sprinkling of pepper to add zest and tang to their flavor. Even garlic, that noxious cousin to the onion, has its uses on occasion, and within reason.

The degree of seasoning required to make food interesting and palatable varies with races and with individuals. Mexican tamales are not to be indulged in lightly or indiscrimately by those who are not used to them, and the quantities of garlic necessary to the well-being of Italians would prove nauseating to an Englishman. Even the taste for such ordinary household ingredients as salt and pepper varies so much among members of the same family, that every dining table offers salt and pepper shakers so that each person may season his food according to his liking.

It is the same with the discords we hear in our music. Some of us like them used sparingly, while others, particularly the young people, want them piping hot. The more dissonances we hear, however, the more accustomed we become to them. Consequently, the development and evolution of music through the centuries has been marked by an increasing use of dissonant combinations. Hermann Helmholtz, the German scientist, wrote that no sharp line can be drawn between consonances and dissonances, aesthetically, because the boundary that separates them changes as tonal systems change in the course of evolution. In other words, the dissonances of yesterday become the consonances of today.

Thus, the use of the term dissonance is elastic. Its most commonly accepted meaning is that of a harsh-sounding combination of sounds, but of course the degree of harshness will vary according to the experience and taste of the listener. The words "consonance" and "dissonance" are derived from the Latin: "consonance" from "consonare"—to sound together, to agree; and "dissonance" from "dissonare"—to sound apart, or disagree in sound. The *Encyclopédie de la Musique du Conservatoire* defines dissonance as "sounding twice," designating "the effect produced by two sounds which seem to repulse each other and give to the ear the impression of two distinct sounds, although struck together."

While musically, or aesthetically, a dissonance is a harsh combination of sounds, in effect it is a chordal combination which so disturbs the ear that it requires satisfaction and appeasement in the chords that follow. The most elementary example of this principle is found in the so-called dominant seventh chord:

If this chord is heard by itself, the musical ear demands something to follow it, something which will answer, or resolve, the unfinished feeling aroused by its dissonance. Thus, the chord is followed by another which pacifies the disturbed musical sense:

The second chord is known as the "resolution" of the first, because it resolves the disturbance the dissonance has caused. When properly resolved, a dissonance is not necessarily unpleasant, it affords contrast to the more comfortable sounds. This brings to mind the man who said that the most wonderful sensation in the world is a good itch—if you can scratch it.

Hearing the first chord alone is like having a man upstairs drop one shoe without the other. A story is told of a music pupil who wanted to revenge himself upon his teacher. After the teacher was in bed, the pupil played the first of the chords on the piano, and hid behind the curtains to see what would happen. In ten or fifteen minutes the teacher groped his way down the stairs, stumbled into the music room, and finding the piano keyboard, struck the second chord. Then, muttering to himself, he went back to bed.

It is in this matter of resolutions that we find a fundamental difference between the music of the old masters and that of modern times. The older composers used dissonances, plenty of them, but they were almost invariably resolved by consonances. Modernists use dissonances alone, and deny the listener's ear the relief of conventional resolutions. Dr. Burney, the eighteenth century music historian, wrote in 1770 that discord "seems to be as much the essence of music, as shade is in painting." He qualified his observation by stating that *provided the ear be at length made amends,* there are few dissonances too strong for it."

In the first Prelude of his *Well-Tempered Clavichord,* Bach wrote a chord which would suit the purpose of almost any present-day composer:

He followed it, however, with two chords of resolution which give the ear its satisfaction:

In the following passage from Bizet's *Le Carillon* (from the *L'Arlesienne* Suite, No. 1) the composer used a particularly biting dissonance at the point marked A, which is not fully resolved until the point marked B is reached in the following measure:

The satisfaction from the eventual resolution is complete, however, even though it was delayed.

Wagner developed a type of dissonance which was

severely attacked at first, but which soon became such an accepted part of the musical vocabulary that it is difficult to understand why it was ever considered dissonant. The technical term for this innovation was "chromaticism," or chromatic harmonies. This is an accurate phrase for describing these chords, for they add considerable color to music, and they vastly increased Wagner's powers of emotional expression.

The basis of chromatic harmonies is a constant changing of key in a musical passage; a passing from one key to another which is known as "modulation." Technically, a chromatic melody or harmonic progression is one which uses tones foreign to the key in which it is written. A melody or harmonic progression which remains in its own key is called a "diatonic" melody, or progression. Thus, a diatonic melody in the key of C major is one which uses no tones except those represented by the white keys on a piano keyboard. If, however, an F sharp is introduced, that is a chromatic tone, and the melody and the accompanying harmony become chromatic, since F sharp does not belong in the key of C.

A striking example of Wagner's chromaticism is found in the opening measures of the Prelude to *Tristan und Isolde:*

Although the key signature of this passage contains no sharps and flats, showing that it is written in the key of A minor, there is only one chord in these first seven measures which properly belongs in that key (the final chord in the third measure). In fact, the key signature of A minor remains unchanged for the first forty-three measures of the Prelude, although the music is actually in that key at only a few places, and then only momentarily.

After Wagner, the composer to cause the greatest furor and disturbance among music-lovers and critics was Richard Strauss, born in 1864 and still living, although his most significant work was completed considerably more than a quarter of a century ago. In his tone-poems Strauss was something of a realist, using descriptive and highly discordant effects to portray the scandalous adventures and horrible end of *Till Eulenspiegel,* and to lend dramatic force to others of his musical narratives. He opened the way to a flood of dissonance from his followers which at first seemed terrifying, but which has gradually become so assimilated by music-lovers that Strauss no longer seems a modernist. At the end of *Also sprach Zarathustra,* another of his tone-poems, he introduced an effect which was highly novel at the time: having the bass instruments sound a chord in one key, and the upper instruments a chord in another key, so closely together that the ear actually hears the two chords at the same time. This was a forerunner of a device known as "polytonality," which will be discussed in more detail in a later chapter.

Strauss was born in Munich. His father was first horn player at the Munich court opera, and his mother came from a family of wealthy Bavarian brewers who were distinguished patrons of the arts. The young Richard was a musical prodigy from early childhood; he started composing at the age of six, and by the time he was ten he had two published works to his credit. At sixteen he composed a symphony and a year later a string quartet.

His early works were written in a classic-romantic

style which derived directly from the Schumann-Brahms school. These included his *Burleske* for piano and orchestra, a symphonic fantasy, *Aus Italien,* and a violin sonata. *Aus Italien* encountered considerable opposition from contemporary musicians; it was considered extremely audacious, particularly for the "vulgarity" of introducing the popular song, *Funiculì, funiculà.* Strauss, incidentally, thought it was a folksong and did not know that Luigi Denza had composed it as recently as 1880, to celebrate the opening of the funicular railway on Mount Vesuvius.

The following years, 1887–89, saw the production of the first of Strauss's orchestral tone-poems which marked the beginning of his truly distinctive contributions to music. These were *Macbeth, Don Juan,* and *Tod und Verklärung.* With *Macbeth,* Strauss started his development and expansion of the Liszt type of programmatic tone-poem. He brought greater musical significance to the form, and employed vivid realism in his descriptive effects. From 1895 to 1898 he produced a tone-poem each year, starting with *Till Eulenspiegel's lustige Streiche* (*Till Eulenspiegel's Merry Pranks*). *Till* is undoubtedly Strauss's orchestral masterpiece; it is not the most elaborate and imposing of the tone-poems, but it has the most freshness and spontaneity.

Each of the other orchestral works from these four years met severe criticism. *Also sprach Zarathustra* was based on Nietzsche's book of that name, and it shared the charges against the original as subversive and anarchistic. *Don Quixote* was attacked for its attempts at realism—the bleating of sheep and a wind-machine—while *Ein Heldenleben* (*The Life of a Hero*), a musical autobiography, was considered the height of bad taste. Who was Strauss to consider himself a hero? The shrieking dissonance of the battle-scene from *Ein Heldenleben* was a peppery dish for the 1890's, while the "adversaries" episode, in which Strauss expressed musically his opinion of music critics, was considered savage and vitriolic.

Ein Heldenleben was the last of the tone-poems to achieve true greatness; the *Sinfonia domestica* (1903), autobiographical in depicting the home and family life of the composer, was skillful and complex, but it showed a lamentable decline in Strauss's inventiveness. The later *Alpensinfonie* (1915) is still less musically important. It is elaborate and grandiose, but pitifully lacking in new ideas.

Strauss has also gained leading distinction as a composer of operas. His first music-drama, *Guntram,* was produced in 1894 at Weimar, with the composer's future wife, Pauline de Ahna, in the leading role. The score and libretto, both written by Strauss, showed that in those years he was an ardent Wagnerian. The second opera, *Feuersnot,* was a setting of a libretto by Ernst von Wolzogen. When it was first produced in Dresden in 1901, it aroused considerable moral indignation because of its plot. In 1905, when *Salome* was produced at Dresden, people began to assume that Strauss was fond of subjects of a decadent nature. *Salome* uses a German translation of Oscar Wilde's play, and musically it was the first of Strauss's operatic masterpieces. When it was produced at the Metropolitan in New York in the season of 1906–07, the directors were so offended by the dance of the seven veils, that they commanded Heinrich Conried, the managing director, to take it from the repertoire after a single performance. In 1909, the shrewd Oscar Hammerstein produced the opera at the Manhattan Opera House with Mary Garden in the leading role. Public curiosity over the lascivious dance was so great that the huge theatre was filled to capacity at doubled prices.

Strauss's next opera went still further in bloodcurdling effects. This was *Elektra,* in which Hugo von Hofmannsthal's libretto gives modern psychological treatment to the ancient Greek legend of Orestes returning to avenge Agamemnon. Where Strauss had mixed decadent luxury with horror in *Salome,* he now piled horror upon horror against a background of persistent gloom and despair. The music was utterly shocking to the ears of 1909; it caused a sensation as the last word in ear-splitting dissonance. It was recognized, however, that the composer had not indulged in discords for their own sake, but was rather investing a scabrous theme with an entirely appropriate musical dress.

Salome and *Elektra* are one-act operas. The next opera, again to a libretto by Hofmannsthal, was a full-length work in three acts. *Der Rosenkavalier,* first produced in 1911, is entirely different in character from its predecessors. The libretto is considered one of the finest operatic texts that has ever been written, and the music, while sometimes heavy and over-complex, is so glamorous and masterful that *Der Rosenkavalier* has become a favorite in the repertoire of opera-houses the world over. It is also the composer's final great work, for he had completed the last of his best orchestral works with *Ein Heldenleben* thirteen years earlier, in 1898, and from 1911 even his operas show a decline in fertility of invention and in musical ideas.

It is not that Strauss has been inactive, he has been more prolific than he was before. The nine operas composed since *Rosenkavalier* include, among others, *Ariadne auf Naxos* (1912) and *Die Aegyptische Helena* (1928), widely produced, but showing that the composer had become musically bankrupt.

Strauss's own high opinion of his works has not declined, and as far as those that came from his prime are concerned, there is no reason why it should, for the public continues to agree. When he visited America for the second time, in 1922, I was assigned to interview him for a music magazine. In the course of the conversation we discussed the future possibilities of music, and the mediums that were open to composers. I asked him whether he felt that melodic originality was still possible; if the available combinations of twelve scale tones could still be arranged to provide new themes and motives, or whether originality in the future would have to take the form of new harmonic treatment of older melodies. His reply was brief and to the point: "Haven't my works," he said, "proved that melodic originality is still possible?"

Strauss's dissonances are commonplaces today, because the sounds that were harsh to the ears of our forefathers, and to our own ears a few decades ago, are not as harsh as they seemed at first. We actually need more seasoning in our music, and for that reason good old Papa Haydn does not provide an altogether satisfying musical menu for twentieth century ears, particularly if his symphonies and quartets are heard alone, without more recent works on the same program. They haven't enough salt and pepper.

Gradually through the centuries, the aural mechanism and the taste of the music-loving public have become used to the new and the strange, for if innovations prove in time to be artistically valid, if they really add to the expressiveness of music, they are ultimately accepted. So each era has accustomed itself to a new set of discords, and people have come actually to demand them. Carl Engel wrote some understanding words on this subject: [1] "Each new tonal device was an innovation in its day," he explained, "designed to communicate to the ear a fresh equivalent of the stimulus necessary to relieve satiety by way of variety. . . . The proportion of discords needed to tauten our nerves depends upon the individual and the generation. . . . In contemporary music we have learned to demand discord not merely for the sake of contrast, but for itself, as an indispensable stimulus."

We must realize, of course, that the harshness of dissonance is tempered by the musical texture which results from the distinctive tone of the instrument, or

[1] In "Harking Back and Looking Forward," *Musical Quarterly*, Jan., 1928.

combinations of instruments, which produce it. Tones of the same pitch will have an entirely different texture when played by a group of string instruments, or by wood winds, than when they are produced by striking the keys of a piano. When we try on the piano an orchestral or chamber music passage and find the combinations of tones biting and metallic, we must remember that the same passage will give an entirely different effect when the tone-combinations are blended by the tone-color of other instruments. It is for this reason that piano transcriptions of modern orchestral works are rarely satisfactory; the tone-color of a percussion instrument is so unlike that of orchestral combinations.

At the risk of becoming technical, it may help towards an understanding of modern music to compare the human conception of musical consonance and dissonance with a few acoustical principles. The art of music, and the practice of harmony, have been developed according to what has pleased human ears; they have been evolved by musicians, not by scientists. Nevertheless, as one compares the growth of the art of music, and the extension of its basic principles, with the laws of acoustics, he finds an interesting parallel between the two. In other words, men have found most pleasing to their ears the combinations of those tones which bear certain physical relationships to each other, even though they may not have been aware that those relationships existed.

All sound is caused by vibration. What we call a noise is produced by irregular vibration; a musical tone by a regular vibration which may be counted and timed. The rate of vibration determines the pitch; the faster the vibration, the higher the tone. At standard pitch, the tone of the A above middle C is produced by a vibration at the rate of 440 impulses a second. The A an octave below vibrates at the rate of 220 a second, or half as fast; while the A an octave above has 880 vibrations a second, or twice as many.

A musical tone reaches the ear through the vibration of the atmosphere, which is set in motion by the vibration of a string (in the case of stringed instruments and of the vocal chords of human beings), or by a vibrating column of air (in the case of wind instruments). Neither the strings nor the columns of air, however, vibrate as a whole throughout the entire duration of the vibration; they break into vibrating segments which produce what are known as "overtones," or subsidiary tones of higher pitch. Sometimes these are called "harmonics" or "upper partials." The ear hears these overtones even though it does not distinguish them and recognizes only the pitch of the principal tone. Overtones lend an instrument or voice its distinctive tone-quality. The flute produces the fewest overtones of any instrument, therefore it has the purest tone, but one that is not particularly colorful.

You yourself can conduct an interesting experiment in overtones at the piano keyboard. Press down the key of C an octave below middle C, without sounding the tone. Hold it down while you strike sharply the C *two* octaves below middle C. Be sure not to press the damper pedal. For an instant you will hear the tone you have actually struck, but as it quickly dies away, you will hear the tone from the key you didn't strike, but for which you are raising the damper and allowing the string to vibrate. The sound you hear is caused by the upper C vibrating in so-called sympathetic vibration with the note you struck. The higher C is the first overtone of the lower C. When you struck the lower C, its overtone caused the air to vibrate at a certain rate, and started the string tuned to that pitch vibrating on its own account.

Now hold down, without sounding the tone, the G below middle C. Strike the low C in the same manner, and you'll hear the tone of G, not as clearly as you heard the upper C, but clearly enough to distinguish it. Then repeat the experiment with the E above middle C, and you'll have the same result, still fainter, but audible.[2]

What you have actually been doing in these experiments is to follow the series of natural overtones, sometimes known as the Harmonic Series. This is represented in musical notation by the following table:

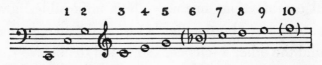

Overtones 6 and 10, enclosed in parentheses, are not perfectly represented by the notes on the staff. Overtone 6 is somewhat lower, or flatter, than B flat, and 10 is about halfway between F and F sharp.

In your experiment, you produced at the start the first overtone of C: the C an octave higher. Next, you produced the second overtone, G. We omitted the third overtone, because that was another C. The fourth overtone, which was considerably fainter, was E. With these three overtones, C, G, and E, you have sounded the three tones which produce the common chord of C:

[2] If you have a grand piano, you can also get an extremely faint tone from B flat.

It has already been stated that musicians were not aware of acoustic principles when they first started to sing and play in parts; music as an art was developed according to the dictates of taste rather than according to scientific ratios and laws. Also, authorities differ as to the actual connection between the so-called harmonic series of overtones and the development of tonal combinations in music. It is impossible, however, to ignore the parallel between the two, one an art and the other a science, and to fail to observe that the tones which have been accepted by Western ears as producing agreeable, or consonant, sounds in combination with other given tones, have corresponded roughly with the natural overtones of those given tones. Moreover, the order in which these tones have come into the musical vocabulary forms an almost identical pattern with the harmonic series.

Thus, the first interval to be accepted as consonant was the octave, and when the Greeks sang in parts they merely sang an octave above or below the melody. An "interval," incidentally, is the distance between two tones, measured by the ratio between the vibrating rate of the two tones; or, in musical notation, by the number of steps on the staff line.[3]

---

[3] For convenience, the piano keyboard may be used for computing intervals. Use the scale of C major, which is represented by the eight white keys starting with middle C, or, for that matter,

The history of music records attempts at harmony from as early as the ninth century. Harmony, of course, is the simultaneous sounding of two or more tones, producing what we know as a chord. In written or printed music, a chord, or harmonic combination, is shown in a vertical arrangement of notes:

In the earliest attempts at harmony, the only intervals which were considered consonant were the octave, the fourth and the fifth. Again consulting the overtone series, we will note that just as the octave is the first natural overtone, the fifth is number 2. In the tempered scale, the fourth is the same as the fifth, by inversion. In other words, while the interval from C to G is a fifth, if we put the G below the C, instead of above it, we have a fourth, computing downwards from G to C:

---

with any C, and ending with the C an octave above. An interval is computed by counting both the lower and upper tones of the interval, as well as those between. Thus, the interval from C to the D above it is a second; we counted two keys, C and D. From C to E is a third, for we counted three keys, C, D, E. Similarly, from C to F is a fourth; from C to G a fifth; from C to A a sixth; from C to B a seventh; and from C to the upper C an eighth, or octave. Continuing further, from middle C to the D above the next higher C is a ninth.

The crude harmony of the ninth century consisted of singing in parts which were an octave, a fourth, or a fifth, from the principal melody. This was known as "organum," which would look something like this in modern notation:

etc.

The chief development of organum was the acceptance of overtone 2 (the fifth and its inversion) as forming a consonant harmonic interval with the basic tone.

You will notice that the parts in organum moved in parallel motion to each other; when the melody proceeded upward or downward in the scale, the accompanying parts moved in the same direction. Two or three hundred years after organum was developed, a new style came into vogue. This was known as "descant," in which the voices moved in both parallel and contrary motion, and thus achieved a greater independence:

etc.

This eventually led to a horizontal type of part-writing which has become known as "counterpoint." Counterpoint is the combination of two or more melodies in a horizontal pattern, in contrast to harmony in which the tones are arranged in vertical combination. Counterpoint produces harmony, however, for the tones of each component melody produce a vertical combination with whichever tones of the other melodies occur simultaneously. If you can persuade one of your friends to sing Dvořák's *Humoresque* while you sing Foster's *Old Folks at Home* you will produce counterpoint. The two melodies go well together because their succession of tones happens to be so arranged that each makes a consonance with the tone of the other at the principal points at which they fall together.

Counter melodies in orchestrations are a form of counterpoint, as also are obbligati which are played simultaneously with the principal melodies of a composition. In fact, it is counterpoint which enriches and lends interest to the instrumental, or choral, arrangement of any work. In orchestral or band pieces the wood-winds, brass instruments and strings, are constantly given decorative passages and added melodies which offer variety as well as richness to the combined effect. One of the most skillful arrangers of musical comedy scores, Robert Russell Bennett, has written an article [4] about scoring for theatre orchestra in which he states:

"Taking anything from a whistled melody to a piano sketch from its author to the lighted orchestra pit of a theatrical production demands a great many things besides theatrical training; but if I were asked what the greatest asset one can have in this work is, I should have to answer, 'counterpoint.' . . . The audience, sitting there watching dimpled knees, and listening to tiny voices singing out familiar intervals in praise of familiar emotions, has no idea what counterpoint is; but let it be stiff, forced, or badly distributed, and the knees become less dimpled, the tiny voices grow tinier, and the general atmosphere becomes charged with an unmistakable *So what?* What the public doesn't know, which is plenty, it very nearly always feels, and that applies to the good things as well as the bad."

[4] *Modern Music,* May–June, 1932.

Another form of counterpoint is the so-called "imitative" counterpoint, in which various voices or instrumental parts imitate and echo each other by repeating what the others have sung or played. This is the basis of the antiphonal music of anthems and choral works, and it is also the fundamental principle of the "canon" and "fugue." A canon is similar to the round, and is constructed on a melody in which the various phrases may be sounded simultaneously with each other. Thus, in the familiar *Three Blind Mice,* the first group starts singing the opening phrase, "Three blind mice, three blind mice." As it starts the second phrase, "See how they run, see how they run," the next group begins the first phrase, "Three blind mice," etc. Then, when the first group comes to the third phrase, "They all ran after the farmer's wife," the second group sings the second phrase, and a third group starts at the beginning. If there are still more singers, as many as six groups may participate, each entering with the opening phrase as the earlier groups come to the successive phrases: "Who cut off their tails with a carving knife"; "You never saw such a sight in your life," and the final, "As three blind mice."

A fugue is a more involved and complicated development of the canon. The term is derived from the Latin *fuga,* meaning a flight, which aptly characterizes the chasing of one part by another, as each echoes and imitates what the other has played or sung. Each instrumental or vocal part in a fugue is equal in importance. The principal theme is first announced by one part, and is then taken up successively by the other parts, as the first part continues to unfold the subsequent progress of the theme. Subsidiary themes, and transpositions to different registers, all treated imitatively, render the construction of a fugue a challenging problem to the composer.

In the hands of the seventeenth and eighteenth century composers, notably Bach and Handel, counterpoint became one of the most flexible and intricate devices of musical composition. The mighty fugues of Bach are monuments of musical ingenuity and inventiveness, so masterful in their construction that accustomed listeners never tire of hearing them.

The oldest known canon, or round, is the thirteenth century English song, *Sumer is icumen in,* of which the manuscript, now in the British Museum, came from Reading Abbey, and is believed to date from 1240. The song is not only the oldest known canon, it is also the oldest known harmonized music which is frequently performed today, and the earliest existing composition for six parts. One of the most important features of *Sumer is icumen in* is its employment of the harmonic intervals of the third and sixth. (The sixth, of course, is an inversion of the third, just as the fourth is an inversion of the fifth:

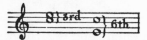

In the early specimens of "descant" the octave and the fifth (or fourth) were still the only intervals that were allowed. With *Sumer is icumen in* a form of descant known as "Fauxbourdon" originated in England, which admitted the interval combinations of the third and sixth. A melody harmonized according to the principles of Fauxbourdon would look like this:

With Fauxbourdon, then, overtone 4 was accepted as a consonant interval. It had required over thirteen hundred years, almost a millennium and a half, for the human ear to become accustomed to the combination of three tones which make the simplest chord in the music of the Western world!

With the acceptance of the third and sixth as consonant intervals, the principle of building chords in thirds came into practice. The common chord, or triad, consists of three tones, of which the upper two are arranged as a series of thirds above the fundamental tone:

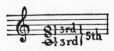

In this chord each tone is a third removed from its neighbor, while the top tone, G, is a fifth from the basic tone, C.

The next step in harmonic development was the introduction of the tone which corresponds roughly with overtone 6 in the harmonic series, and which is a seventh removed from the fundamental tone, and also a third above the fifth:

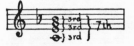

This was indeed a radical departure. Even though the harmonic interval of the seventh was well established by the time of Claudio Monteverdi (sixteenth and seventeenth centuries), it was still considered a dissonance, and its use was limited by rigid rules and limitations. Most of the protests which Monteverdi's music provoked were caused by his free use of seventh chords.

The principle of building chords in thirds was advanced principally by a French composer, Jean

Philippe Rameau (1683–1764). Rameau also increased the variety of the harmonic vocabulary by discovering that the common chord may be "inverted" by using another of its tones than the fundamental as the lowest tone of the chord. Thus the common chord of C has E for its lowest tone in its first inversion:

and G for its lowest tone in its second inversion:

Throughout the entire history of music, the extension of the harmonic vocabulary has consisted largely of adding another third to previously existing chords. In modern music composers make free use of chords of the ninth, and the eleventh, and others with even further added thirds:

Again, comparison with the table of overtones (page 57) shows an interesting parallel. In the foregoing example, the ninth and eleventh intervals of the chords (D and F) are next in the series of overtones after the seventh (B flat), omitting, of course, overtones 7 and 9 (C and E), which are repetitions, in higher octaves, of lower overtones. Thus, the acceptance of intervals which had formerly been considered dissonant, has continued to have its approximate counterpart in the series of natural harmonics, from early times to the present.

The harmonic intervals of the ninth and the eleventh (and, in modern music, the thirteenth) have not had any easier a time in finding acceptance than their predecessors—the fifth, third, and seventh. Although all of them are now in common use, they have, to quote Aaron Copland in *Our New Music*,[5] "only gradually fought their way into the musical sun, and each time, a minor revolution had to take place before they were admitted."

While it is neither necessary nor desirable that these pages should present a detailed exposition of the principles of traditional harmony and counterpoint, there are certain matters the reader should have in

[5] New York: Whittlesey House, 1941.

mind, particularly in comparing modern music with that of earlier times. When we learn that composers have violated or disregarded the rules that limited their predecessors, it will help matters materially if we know what some of those rules were.

The art of harmony deals not only with chords, but, even more important, with the progression of chords; in other words, with the succession of tone-combinations and the way in which the several tones of a chord proceed to those of the following chord. These principles of harmonic progression apply also to counterpoint, for while counterpoint is a horizontal combination, or weaving together, of independent melodies, it actually produces harmonic combinations when tones of the separate melodies are heard together.

The pupil studying harmony has traditionally been confronted with a series of "don'ts," rules which he must not violate when he is writing what is called "strict" harmony or counterpoint. The most famous of these rules is that no harmonic progression should contain parallel fifths between any two voices. In short, the composer must not write progressions which were used in ninth-century organum. The following passage would be "incorrect";

because the progression of the G to A in an upper part forms so-called parallel fifths with the progression of C to D in the bass. The two tones were a fifth apart in the first chord, and each moved upward, in the same direction, to form another fifth in the following chord. To be "correct," the progression should have been written:

This avoids the parallel fifths. Similarly, parallel octaves between two parts were forbidden. These rules were broken on occasion, of course, but unless a composer violated them consciously, to produce an intended effect, he was considered unqualified for his profession.

The use of seventh chords, and of their dissonant intervals, has been governed by well-defined rules, which provide for their resolution and also for their preparation through the chords which precede them. The use of other dissonant tones has also been regulated. Consequently, the traditional rules specify not only what combinations of tones may be used, but what their relationship shall be to the chords that precede and follow them. As the rules have been liberalized and the restrictions have relaxed, further dissonances have been permitted, and composers have been permitted to use them with increasing freedom and independence.

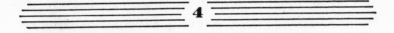

DEBUSSY STARTS SOMETHING—

IMPRESSIONISM

To TWENTIETH-CENTURY music lovers, the works of
Claude Debussy (1862–1918) mark the beginning of
modern music. His harmonic devices were so different from those of earlier music that they necessitated
the re-writing of many harmony text-books, while the
mood and atmosphere of his music proved so novel
that it was baffling to many on first hearing. In addition, Debussy himself was such a free-thinker that he
delighted in defying convention, and no doubt enjoyed the discomfiture of his teachers. He subscribed
to the radical idea that the composer's ear, and taste,
provided a better standard of what is effective than
the rules of harmony and counterpoint.

Debussy brought to music a style which is known as
impressionism, a direct outgrowth of impressionistic

art and literature. Impressionism deals with the effect of objects, rather than objects themselves. The term was first applied derisively to the work of a group of painters which was headed by Claude Monet in France. In addition to Monet, the impressionist painters included Manet, Degas, Renoir, Pissarro and Cézanne. As early as 1867 Monet exhibited a painting which he called *Impression: Rising Sun*. Visitors to the gallery who expected to see a realistic image of a sunrise were dumfounded to behold what the artist called "the fugitive changes of nature."

Impressionistic art substitutes for a photographic representation of what the eye actually sees, the emotional reaction of the artist to the scene he is painting. It gives a mental image, the sensation aroused by a landscape, a figure, or an object; it is not concerned with reproducing concrete or tangible things. In the same manner, the symbolist poets, such writers as Stéphane Mallarmé, use words, not for their meaning, but for their sound, as symbols to suggest moods.

Debussy's doubting nature, his inborn habit of questioning the reason for customs, no matter how respectable, made it inevitable that he should be a revolutionary, and his association with impressionistic artists and writers led him to evolve a similar style in music. He left us a body of works that are marked by shimmering beauty, by vague, filmy, atmospheric effects, hued with delicate tints rather than solid colors.

Impressionism is a reaction against realism, and also against the soaring romanticism of such composers as Richard Wagner. It is, however, directly derived from romanticism, for it deals with sensations and with sentiment. It differs from romanticism in abjuring the grand manner; it has nothing of bombast, and instead of offering heroics, it concerns itself with veiled, mystic half-shadows.

Although impressionism is almost the direct opposite of realism, it was the work of a realist composer, the Russian Modeste Moussorgsky (1839–1881), which exercised the greatest influence on Debussy as a free-thinker in his music. That was, perhaps, because Moussorgsky represented a complete breaking away from Wagnerism; for while Debussy was an ardent Wagnerite in his youth he came to feel that French music must rid itself of the German romantic influence if it was to be vital and independent.

Moussorgsky was a musically uncouth, rugged pioneer, concerned primarily with writing music which would be natural and sincere. Inadequately trained, according to conservatory standards, he escaped the German and Italian influences that dominated the late nineteenth century Russian composers, including, of course, Tschaikowsky. Moussorgsky grew primarily from Russian folk-songs, rhythmically and melodically. His harmonic treatment of this material came not from text-books, but from the modal style of the Greek Catholic church. He did not necessarily question the established rules of harmony, for it is doubtful that he knew them intimately; he proceeded on the basis that his own ear and musical instinct would lead him to what was appropriate and effective. This resulted in an harmonic freedom which has set a precedent for the modern composers of a later day.

It is not known exactly when Debussy first became familiar with Moussorgsky's work; probably not when he was himself in Russia as musical tutor in the establishment of Baroness von Meck (1880–82). His first acquaintance with the music of the Russian composer came later, but he was always ready to express his debt to Moussorgsky. They had much in common: a disregard for academic convention, a yearning to be natural and simple, and a high respect for truth in art. Once Debussy remarked that anyone who heard Moussorgsky's opera, *Boris Godounov*, would hear the whole of his own *Pelléas et Mélisande*.

Fundamentally, there was a wide difference in the

approach of the two artists to their problems. Moussorgsky had little training, so he could not be said to have broken rules and traditions consciously. He proceeded largely by instinct, and disregarded convention without being aware of its existence. Debussy was trained rigidly at the Paris Conservatoire. He learned the rules and then consciously revolted against their restrictions. Whatever he violated, he did so consciously and intentionally.

His revolt began in his student days at the Conservatoire. To his fellow pupils he complained about the strict rules they were compelled to observe—resolving seventh chords and dissonances; avoidance of parallel fifths and octaves; writing parts in contrary, rather than parallel, motion. He conducted experiments of his own: devising chord combinations which sounded like the bells he had heard in his childhood; adding to his chords the intervals of the ninth and the eleventh; making dissonances that were explained by no other reason than that Debussy liked them that way.

His extraordinary talents won him the Prix de Rome in 1884, but his works departed so radically from accepted custom that they shocked the judges when he sent them home from Italy. The climax was reached when he refused to write the accustomed overture for the concert devoted annually to the works by the prize winner. The concert of Debussy works was not given.

This crisis occurred in 1890, and from that time Debussy turned from his musical colleagues, and sought the companionship of painters and artists who were following impressionist ideas. His disillusionment regarding Wagner became complete on a second visit to Bayreuth in 1889, and though he still admitted the tremendous power of Wagner's genius, he came to feel that it would stifle those who sought to follow it. He grew more and more consciously French in his viewpoint, and came to refer to himself as "musicien français."

He had already produced his *L'Enfant Prodigue*, the cantata which won for him the Prix de Rome in 1884, and *La Damoiselle éleu* (1887–88); but his first really challenging works were the String Quartet (1893) and his *Prélude à l'Après-midi d'un faune*, after Mallarmé's poem (1894). In 1900 two of his Nocturnes for orchestra were first performed— *Nuages* and *Fêtes*, and in the following year the third of them was heard—*Sirenes*. In 1902 he completed and produced the work he had been laboring on for ten years, an opera on Maeterlinck's poem, *Pelléas et Mélisande*.

Pelléas is generally acknowledged to be one of the

great masterpieces of operatic literature, for it provides one of the most expressive settings of a dramatic text that has ever been composed. The handling of the poem is so skillful that the singers can enunciate the words with almost the naturalness of speech. The orchestral background is at all times an integral part of the drama, neither a mere accompaniment nor yet an independent series of symphonic episodes. Finally, the atmospheric mood of the score, restrained and reticent, gives the opera an elusiveness, a mysterious, shadowy spirituality, which makes the pathos and tragedy of the drama poignant and real.

The Maeterlinck drama which Debussy set to such exquisite music tells the story of Mélisande, married to the considerably older Golaud. Inevitably she falls in love with Golaud's younger brother, Pelléas, and finally, in the scene which brings the opera to a climax, the two lovers cast aside their reserve and speak of their love without restraint. The jealous husband watches them, and in a fit of fury kills his brother, Pelléas. In the last act, Mélisande dies after she has given birth to a child.

The tragic story is unfolded, poetically and musically, with a touching tenderness which renders it a moving, delicately wrought love story motivated by authentically human emotions.

In spite of the fact that Debussy made of the drama one of the operatic masterpieces of all time, Maeterlinck was openly hostile to the work. When it was produced at the Paris Opéra-Comique, with Mary Garden as Mélisande, an anonymous pamphlet, denouncing the opera, was distributed outside the opera house during the dress rehearsal. The authorship of this pamphlet was attributed to Maeterlinck. A few weeks before, the poet had published a letter in the magazine, *Le Figaro*, in which he characterized *Pelléas* as "a work which is now strange and hostile to me," and stated: "I can only wish its immediate and emphatic failure."

It was difficult to understand Maeterlinck's attitude, but the generally accepted explanation was that Mary Garden had been chosen for the leading role, rather than a singer whom Maeterlinck later married, Georgette Leblanc.

After *Pelléas et Mélisande*, Debussy's next major work was the tone-poem, *La Mer*, first performed in 1905; and then came the orchestral *Images* (1909–12) which included *Ibéria*. In later years Debussy composed the piano pieces which have become almost as standard in the concert repertoire as those of Chopin: the *Suite Bergamasque* (1890–1905); the *Children's Corner* suite (1906–8); the *Préludes* (Book I, 1910;

Book II, 1910–13); and the book of *Études* (1915).

Debussy's most revolutionary break with tradition lay in his treatment of the individual chord as an indépendent unit. We have already remarked that the science of harmony is concerned largely with the progression of chords, and that its rules govern principally the passage from one chord to another. Debussy looked upon a chord as a color medium which could be entirely independent of anything that came before it or followed it. Thus dissonance became an end in itself, and not merely a temporary disturbance of the ear which must be set at rest by a consonance. When Debussy wrote dissonant chords he had little thought of resolving them, for his chords were entities which he could arrange in any way his taste dictated.

He could never understand why parallel consecutive fifths were forbidden. He liked the sound of them, even in his student days at the Conservatoire, and through his career he used them frequently. *La Sérénade interrompue*, the ninth Prélude of Book I, has an interesting succession of parallel fifths:

Permission to quote from the Debussy Préludes has been granted by Durand & Cie., Paris, and Elkan-Vogel Co., Inc., Philadelphia, Pa., copyright owners.

Debussy's use of parallel fifths was not always as modern as it seems; sometimes it reverts to mediaeval practices. A number of Debussy's progressions are exactly the same as those of ninth-century organum. In *La Cathédrale engloutie*, the composer paints a picture of a cathedral submerged in fathoms of water, and he gains a mystic, stately effect through the parallel motion of fourths and fifths, identical with organum:

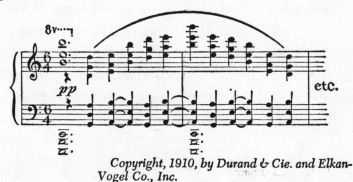

Copyright, 1910, by Durand & Cie. and Elkan-Vogel Co., Inc.

A similar progression is found in another of the Préludes, *La Fille aux chevin de lin* (*The Girl with the Flaxen Hair*):

Copyright, 1910, by Durand & Cie. and Elkan-Vogel Co., Inc.

Debussy's use of ninth chords is one of the devices most closely associated with his work. The ninth chord, as we found in the preceding chapter, is formed by adding another tone to the seventh chord, the added tone being a third higher than the seventh (see pages 67–68). The ninth chord is distinguished by its questioning character, and if the chord is unresolved, the ear is left with an unsatisfied problem. The result is a shadowy impression; cryptic, impenetrable.

Ninth chords are characteristic, not only of Debussy's music, but of the works of all impressionists. In *The White Peacock*, a piano piece by an American impressionist, Charles T. Griffes, an unresolved ninth chord suggests the languorous reserve, the detached hauteur of the proud peacock:

Parallel ninth chords give a peculiarly sliding effect, which has been used in recent years by arrangers of popular music. Ravel employed them effectively in his *Pavane pour une Infante defunte:*

etc.

By kind permission of the copyright owners.

Another Debussyism is the use of the "whole-tone" scale. The whole-tone scale differs from the traditional diatonic scales by having only six steps, instead of seven, and by progressing from step to step, or tone to tone, in equal intervals throughout its octave length. The diatonic scale, in either the major or minor mode, consists of unequal intervals (see pages 45–46). If you examine the notes forming the scale of C major on the piano keyboard, you will find that the intervals between E and F, and between B and C, are smaller than the others in the scale. These half-steps give the diatonic scale a definite shape, and lead to a definite resting place.

The whole-tone scale is formed in this fashion:

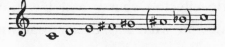

Since all the intervals, or spaces between the tones, are equal, there are no smaller intervals to establish a temporary or final resting place. Melodies and harmonies built on the whole-tone scale are therefore vague and indefinite, and suggest mistiness and wraith-like shadows.

The most consistent use Debussy made of the whole-tone scale is found in the second Prélude of Book I, *Voiles*. All except six measures of this piece are constructed on a whole-tone pattern. The opening measures start:

In addition to devices which may be analyzed according to harmonic principles, Debussy and the other impressionists have added to their chords dissonant tones which cannot be satisfactorily explained by analysis. They are apparently inserted for the reason that the composers liked the sound they produced, or that they were necessary for the descriptive or atmospheric effect. Debussy and his disciples also experimented in what has become known as polytonality, or the use of more than one key at the same time. These experiments were only preliminaries to the polytonal techniques which are discussed in a later chapter, and they consisted chiefly of sudden modulations, or changes of key, which give the ear the impression of hearing the several keys, or tonalities, simultaneously. Sometimes chords in a key foreign to the passage are inserted, and give a similar effect.

The impressionists also sought freedom and flexibility of rhythm. In Debussy's first Prélude in Book I, *Danseuses de Delphes*, the time-signature changes irregularly throughout the piece from $\frac{3}{4}$ to $\frac{4}{4}$. The last Prélude of Book II, *Feux d'artifice*, begins with a time-signature of $\frac{4}{8}$. After the first thirty-one measures, the time-signature changes with each measure: $\frac{2}{8}$, $\frac{4}{8}$, $\frac{3}{8}$, $\frac{4}{8}$. Then the $\frac{4}{8}$ continues for five measures, and is interrupted by a single measure in $\frac{5}{8}$. In the third movement of his Sonatine for piano, Ravel used alternately four different time-signatures: $\frac{3}{4}$, $\frac{5}{4}$, $\frac{4}{4}$, and $\frac{2}{4}$.

These are only a few of the basic methods Debussy and his followers have developed, and it must not be assumed that they represent the sum total of the impressionist technique. Nevertheless, the devices Debussy used are so distinctive and so readily recognized, that they are perhaps more closely associated with his name than the idiom of any other composer. They have put his disciples at a considerable disadvantage, for when other composers use the whole-tone scale and ninth chords they often seem to be merely imitating their greater model.

A composer who exerted a deep influence on Debussy was a fellow-Frenchman, Erik Satie (1866–1925). Satie and Debussy first met when Satie was earning a meager living as a pianist in a Montmartre cabaret. The two musicians struck up a close friendship, and would sit up for long hours after the café had closed, discussing their ideas and problems. These conversations did much to clarify Debussy's ideas, and it is said that it was Satie who first suggested to Debussy that he make an opera from *Pelléas et Mélisande.*

In his youth, Satie had little musical training. In 1883 he spent a miserable year at the Paris Conservatoire, but his rebellious nature and his love for sounds that others considered ugly made him leave his teachers before he finished his prescribed studies. He accordingly went his own way, and wrote unorthodox piano pieces to which he gave grotesque and satirical titles: *Cold Pieces; Pointed Arches; Pieces in the Form of a Pear; Unpleasant Glances;* and others equally absurd.

This type of satire gained for Satie a wide reputation as a humorist, although the humor was more often in the titles than in the music. When he was forty years old he decided that he was handicapped by lack of training, and he entered the Schola Cantorum in Paris, where he studied with d'Indy and Roussel for three years. The rigid discipline to which Satie subjected himself did not, however, destroy his individuality.

In a way, Satie was a crusader. He was against anything in music that took itself too seriously; he lampooned anybody or anything which smacked of what we today would call "stuff-shirtedness." Consequently he avoided whatever seemed impressive, and by writing in a naïvely simple manner he caused his detractors to call him trifling and trivial.

Although he achieved a wide reputation in his day, Satie has proved more important for his influence on other composers than for his own works. He not only helped Debussy to work out his impressionist ideas, he was also an important factor in the development of other French composers, particularly the so-called "Group of Six" who are discussed in a later chapter.

There are many other composers who either had an artistic kinship with Debussy, or proved to be his disciples by becoming impressionists. Paul Dukas (1865–1935), the French composer known principally for his orchestral scherzo, *L'Apprenti Sorcier*, was, like Debussy, far removed from the realism that was so prevalent during his youth. His work was marked by symbolism, and a typically French delicacy of sentiment. Florent Schmitt, born in Blâmont, France, in 1870, is perhaps more grandiose than Debussy in his larger works, but in his chamber music, particularly in his Quintet for Piano and Strings, he is distinctly an impressionist.

Next to Debussy, Maurice Ravel (1875–1937) has perhaps been the most widely performed of modern French composers. Certainly, his *Bolero,* for orchestra, has achieved a vogue that has had few competitors. In a number of his works Ravel undeniably used methods that have characterized the impressionists; but it is not only as an impressionist that we shall meet Ravel. Unlike Debussy, he remained fundamentally a classicist, even though he adopted modern methods and was something of an experimenter on his own account. Ravel used the whole-tone scale very little, and although he made frequent use of the ninth chord, he was more fond of the chord of the eleventh. Also, as we shall discover, he was often a polytonalist.

England has produced a number of impressionists. Frederick Delius (1862–1934), like Debussy, was more closely akin to poets and painters than to musicians. A number of his early years were spent in

America, on an orange grove in Florida, and he once remarked to his biographer, Eric Fenby, that through sitting and gazing at nature, in Florida, he gradually learned the way in which he would eventually find himself. He evolved a style distinctly his own, aimed not so much at movement and action as at sensuous meditation. Cyril Scott (1879–) is distinctly impressionistic in the delicate tints of his harmonic structure; in fact, some of his piano pieces and songs won Debussy's praise. Scott's vogue, however, has waned considerably in recent years, and his music has become interesting chiefly because of its experimental character.

Others of the English impressionists are Frank Bridge (1879–), Gustav Holst (1874–1934), John Ireland (1879–), and Eugene Goossens (1893–), who, since 1923, has been active chiefly in America. Also, Ralph Vaughan Williams (1872–), considered today the dean of British composers, showed the influence of French impressionism in his early works. Williams, however, is more closely identified with welding English folk-songs into a truly British idiom.

In Italy the leading impressionists have been the late Ottorino Respighi (1879–1936), with his symphonic poems, *Pines of Rome* and *Fountains of Rome*, and Alfredo Casella (1883–). Spain has had Isaac

Albéniz (1860–1909), composer of atmospheric piano pieces (the suite *Iberia,* a Tango in D, *Seguidillas,* and others), and Manuel de Falla (1876–   ) whose operas, *La Vida Breve,* and *El Sombrero de Tres Picos* (*The Three-Cornered Hat*) are widely known through orchestral performances of their dances. De Falla was definitely influenced by the modern French school in his orchestral technique.

Poland's leading impressionist was Karol Szymanowski (1883–1937), who was interested in oriental philosophy and mysticism; while Hungary has given us Zoltán Kodály (1882–   ), famous for his comic opera, *Háry János,* and for his impressionistic piano music. In his *Epitaphe,* for piano, Kodály uses a modified form of organum.

Alexander Scriabin, the Russian, started his composing career as a romantic follower of Chopin and Liszt, but as he developed, he shared with Debussy the feeling that the accepted harmonic intervals were not enough to express the modern composer's ideas. Consequently, he too made use of the upper intervals of the eleventh, the thirteenth, and some even higher. He also foreshadowed the atonalists, who are discussed in the following chapter, by arbitrarily building chords in fourths, rather than in thirds. Thus, two piano pieces of his Opus 57 are based on a chord consisting of C, F sharp, B, and E. In his orchestral tone-poem, *Prometheus,* his so-called "mystic" chord is a combination of five fourths, formed by C, F sharp, B flat, E, A, and D.

Scriabin was born in Moscow in 1872. He studied at the Moscow Conservatory (piano with Safonoff and composition with Tanieff), and aroused the interest of the publisher, Belaieff, who not only issued his works on generous terms, but also sponsored an extended European concert tour in which the programs consisted largely of Scriabin's own compositions. Later, in 1908, Scriabin enjoyed the patronage of Sergei Koussevitzky, who at the time was head of the Russian Music Publishing Society. This organization offered him a substantial yearly retainer, and Koussevitsky engaged him for a tour of the Volga cities with his orchestra.

As a composer, Scriabin passed through definitely marked stages of development. At the start, he was strongly influenced by Chopin, and being an excellent pianist himself, he naturally composed a long list of piano pieces. Some of them have become enormously popular, particularly the Études and the Préludes. About the turn of the century he began to evolve his more advanced style, and the harmonic structure of his works became widely discussed. For

(91)

a time he ranked with Debussy as a symbol of modernism, particularly when he came under the influence of a theosophy circle in Brussels in 1908–10, and the mystic strain in his music became more pronounced. His major works reflect this influence, and show him seeking an essential relation between art and religion. In *Prometheus* (1909–10) he conceived an affinity, spiritual as well as scientific, between tone and color, and he made provision for prescribed colors to be thrown on a screen while the music was being performed. The work was only once performed in this manner, however; at Carnegie Hall, New York, in 1914. The results were not sufficiently convincing to warrant repetition.

Scriabin's ardent desire to achieve a perfect synthesis of the arts for the service of religion led him to plan a so-called *Mystery* of mammoth proportions. This was never completed, for he died in 1915 with only the sketches outlined for the introductory movement.

Aside from *Prometheus*, Scriabin's best known orchestral work is the *Poem of Ecstasy*, composed in 1907–08. This symphony, so called, is intended by the composer to set forth the "Joy of Creative Activity." The two basic motives of the Prologue symbolize the composer's "Strife after the Ideal," and a gradual

"Awakening of the Soul." Later themes represent "Human Love" and the "Will to Rise."

Performances of both *Prometheus* and the *Poem of Ecstasy* are becoming less frequent in these times. In some respects it is difficult to understand why they should not be played more often, for they are filled with passages of strange loveliness and mystical effects that seem magic. It may be that harmonically Scriabin stuck too closely to the formulae he devised, so that his style became a series of mannerisms rather than a flexible idiom. Certainly, his harmonies were as bold and daring in their day as those of Debussy, but Debussy rarely allowed his chordal innovations to overshadow his musical and poetic message. When the novelty of Scriabin's patterns had worn off, they began to seem obvious, and public interest started to center in the styles of later composers who were further advanced and still more daring.

Another Russian to show a kinship with the impressionists was Vladimir Rebikoff (1866–1920), a native of Siberia, who graduated from the influence of his countryman, Tschaikowsky, and was one of the first composers to use the whole-tone scale. Rebikoff has been called the father of Russian modernism.

Dozens of composers in the United States have been influenced by French impressionism at one time or another in their careers. The shimmering, sparkling color of the works of Charles Martin Loeffler (1861–1935) make him a close ally of the impressionists. He was profoundly absorbed with Gregorian plain-song, and the church modes of the middle ages. The haunting, brooding strains of his *Pagan Poem* are like strange incense.

Charles Tomlinson Griffes (1884–1920) was at one stage in his life the most definitely impressionistic composer we have yet produced in this country. Although he was at first definitely under the influence of his German teachers, he came to lean toward the modern French school. In his piano works: the tone-pictures—*The Lake at Evening; The Vale of Dreams; The Night Winds,* and the *Roman Sketches—The White Peacock; Nightfall; The Fountain of the Acqua Paola; Clouds*—he was distinctly a Debussy disciple. His reverence for Ravel exceeded his admiration of Debussy, but he delighted so much in individual chord combinations, dependent on nothing that goes before or follows them, and he had such a predilection for modes and Oriental scales, that his kinship with Debussy was complete.

In his early years, Louis Gruenberg (1884–) was decidedly impressionistic, particularly in the piano pieces, Opus 3—*The Temple of Isis; The Sacrifice;*

Dance of the Veiled Women; Night; The Flame Dance of Isis. John Alden Carpenter (1876–) used whole-tone progressions, ninth chords, and other impressionist patterns in his early songs and in the orchestral suite, *Adventures in a Perambulator.* It should be noted, however, that when Carpenter first experimented with these devices, he had not heard a single note of Debussy's music. Ernest Bloch (1880–) has had his impressionist moments, too, even though he has gone far beyond the commonly accepted devices by experimenting with quarter-tones in his Quintet for Piano and Strings. Emerson Whithorne (1884–) becomes an impressionist by being the opposite of a realist. He combines romanticism and impressionism in a manner which shows that the two are closely allied. His symphonic poem, *Dream Pedlar,* is luminous music, and, as Lawrence Gilman remarked, "full of pleasant sounds and fairy evocations."

There are many others, here and abroad. Twenty-five years ago to be a modernist was almost inevitably to be an impressionist. Somewhere around 1920, I can recall taking a piece of my own to a violinist and explaining that it was based on the whole-tone scale. "Of course," he said. Yet, beautiful and delicate as the effects the impressionists gave us have been, they have proved too fragile, too ephemeral, to stand the excessive use to which they were put. The more obvious of them wore themselves out chiefly because they could be adopted so easily; some of them became clichés useful to anyone who could put notes on paper. Even some of Debussy's works have not worn too well. As Aaron Copland has written: [1] "It is his sentimental side that is already wearing thin in many of the lesser works. Despite his musical iconoclasm, Debussy was the hedonistic poet of a thoroughly bourgeois world. There is something cushioned and protected, something velvety-soft and over-comfortable about his music. It reflects a span of life when Europe thought itself most secure, between the years 1870 and 1914. One wonders what the eventual fate of this music will be in the uncertain world ahead. A time may come when it will seem over-refined, decadent, effeminate. But," Copland is careful to add, "no world that we can foresee would ever wish to do without Debussy's music when he is at his best. At such times he is matchlessly poetic and touching and sensitive."

[1] *Our New Music.* New York: Whittlesey House, 1941.

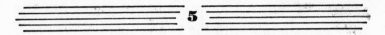

5

SCHOENBERG FINISHES SOMETHING

—ATONALITY

MODERN DEVICES in music have generally been a development and extension of something that has existed before. Debussy's ninth and eleventh chords were the simpler chords of earlier composers to which further tones were added at regular intervals. Wagner's chromaticism was a freer passing from one key to another. The liberties Schumann and Chopin took with established forms were merely extensions of the same forms. Moreover, this evolutionary process has in general followed scientific acoustic principles, even though the innovations were developed by trial and error rather than by laboratory methods.

This explains why atonality is the most difficult of all modern systems for the layman to understand and accept, for it represents a sharp break with what has gone before and what has been developed by slow process. It discards all previous rules and conventions, and starting with the twelve tones of the scale, sets up an entirely new system.

It is not fair to assume that atonal composers have written the way they do haphazardly, or that they compose differently merely because they have not had the patience to master the technique of their craft. To the novice it seems that the same effect could be gained by taking a brush filled with ink and spattering it on a fresh page of music paper. Perhaps the result would be no more difficult to perform or listen to, but the works of the leading atonalists are produced with as much thought and labor as went into the works of the older masters. Whatever drawbacks atonal music may possess generally result from an over-scientific approach, rather than from any lack of workmanship.

The history of atonality is learned best through the career of its leading exponent, Arnold Schoenberg. A native of Vienna, born September 13, 1874, Schoenberg did not decide to be a professional musician until he was sixteen years of age. He had been a devoted amateur, and had enjoyed playing in chamber music ensembles, sometimes composing violin duets, trios, and quartets for the groups he played with. He showed some of his compositions to a Vienna musician named Alexander von Zemlinsky, a friend of Brahms, and Zemlinsky gave Schoenberg the only instruction he ever had, for he is mostly self-taught.

In 1902 Zemlinsky remarked of his pupil: "He knows more than I do now, and what he does not know, he feels. He has a brilliant and an inquiring mind. And he has the greatest amount of sincerity." Meanwhile Schoenberg had been supporting himself by making orchestrations of other composers' operettas, and acting as *Kapellmeister* for a Vienna café. His own compositions in this period included his famous *Verklaerte Nacht,* first composed for string sextet, and later scored for string orchestra; and a symphonic poem for orchestra, *Pelléas und Mélisande.* He had also started his *Gurre-Lieder,* for chorus and orchestra, but the necessity of earning a living kept him from completing it until 1911.

In *Verklaerte Nacht,* Schoenberg showed himself to be a mixture of post-romanticist and impressionist. Having grown up in the midst of the German tradition, he was naturally filled with the intensity of feeling that marked the works of Wagner and the later Bruckner, Mahler and Strauss. For a time Schoenberg gave full expression to this emotionalism, and the tonal beauty of his *Transfigured Night* bathes it in a loveliness that is shimmering and starry.

His "inquiring mind," however, was not satisfied. Like Debussy, Schoenberg felt himself enslaved and shackled by his Wagnerian inheritance, and he determined to be a free man artistically, no matter what it cost him. He decided that the only way he could be free was to break entirely with tradition, to evolve something that would be altogether new, a musical speech that would have in it nothing of the past. And what he devised has compelled the listener, as well as the composer, to revise completely his viewpoint towards music and his conception of tonal beauty and effectiveness.

Opposition arose immediately. When Schoenberg's early works in a new idiom were first performed (the Chamber Symphony and the String Quartet in D minor) the hostile demonstration was so violent that Gustav Mahler stepped to the platform and begged the audience to listen to the rest of the concert. Later, when the Second String Quartet was introduced by the Rosé Quartet, the audience again became riotous.

In spite of hostility, Schoenberg continued his course, and finally perfected his atonal system with his Five Piano Pieces, Opus 23. In these his principles are rigidly applied, more consistently than in his earlier piano pieces or in his melodramatic chamber music composition, *Pierrot Lunaire* (1912). In addition to composing, he has been active as a teacher, giving lessons in conventional harmony and counterpoint, as well as gathering together a group of atonal disciples. A few years ago he came to the United States, and now makes his home in this country.

A literal definition of atonality would be "an absence of the relationship of all the tones and chords to a central keynote." [1] Thus it is the opposite of *tonality*, which, of course, is the principle of key in music, or, to quote Webster: "the character which a composition has by virtue of the relationship of all its tones and chords to the keynote of the whole." In tonal music, a passage in C major revolves about the tone of C, and the ear finds rest and satisfaction when the tone of C, and the chord which has it for its root, are sounded at the close. Instead of having for its basis the major or minor scale of C, or any other key, atonal music is based on a twelve-tone scale, which represents every chromatic tone within the compass

[1] Article on "Atonality" in Oscar Thompson (editor), *The International Cyclopedia of Music and Musicians*. New York: Dodd, Mead & Co.

of an octave, in other words, the tones represented by all the black and white keys on the piano keyboard.

This twelve-tone scale differs from the chromatic scale, however, for in tonal music, the chromatic scale is in effect composed of seven scale degrees and five auxiliary tones. In the key of C, the white keys on the piano represent the seven scale degrees, and the black keys the five auxiliary tones. In atonal music each of the twelve degrees is of equal importance. Instead of having one central key-tone, an atonal passage has twelve independent tonal centers, each having a separate relationship to each of the eleven other tones. Thus, a piece may begin on any of the twelve tones, singly or in combination with any of the others, and may end on any tone or chord combination the composer chooses.

The exponents of atonality resent the term. They claim that their music is not lacking in tonality; far from it, it has *twelve* tonal centers instead of only one. It should, they say, be called "twelve-toned," rather than "atonal" music. Some of them call it "pantonal." Nevertheless, the terms "atonality," and "atonal music" have been so firmly fixed in the vocabulary of music that they are used in spite of the merits of the case.

One of the basic principles of atonal music is condensation of material. In striving to free himself from Wagnerian heroics, Schoenberg felt that there must be no high-flown, long-extended passages in his music. Nor must there be the flowing development sections which composers like Beethoven made an indispensable part of their symphonies. Hence Schoenberg would be laconic, almost monosyllabic in his new music, and he wrote piano pieces a single page in length, some of them containing as few as nine measures each.

He explained this need for brevity in a lecture he delivered in Paris in 1911. "Relinquishment of tonality," he said, "implies a corresponding relinquishment of the structural process founded upon the very principle of tonality; and therefore early examples of works written by means of twelve notes between which no other relationship exists than their relation to one another were necessarily very brief."

Another fundamental principle is the avoidance of consonant combinations, and a rigid insistence on dissonant chords, unrelieved by anything in the way of a simple three-toned triad in thirds, or even a seventh or ninth chord. Thus, atonal music must be written with extreme care to avoid any combinations which would be pleasing to the ear of the man who likes his music sweet. It cannot be composed haphazardly,

(103)

but requires mathematical and studied exactness to produce an uninterrupted succession of harsh sounds.

In his 1911 lecture Schoenberg discussed this necessity for dissonance: "It is likely that, for a time at least, consonant chords will have to disappear from music if the tonal principle is eliminated—not for physical reasons, but for reasons of economy. . . . A tonal consonance asserts its claims on everything that follows it, and regressively on all that came before. Hence, consonant chords tend to occupy an excessive amount of room, and might disturb the balance proper to the new scheme—unless some way is found either of satisfying or of suppressing the requirements of such chords."

In other words, pleasant sounds are objectionable because they cannot stand alone as well as dissonances can, so if atonal composers are going to write short pieces, they must avoid consonances. One of the methods used to produce dissonances has been the construction of chords in fourths, rather than in thirds:

This method of chord construction, we have found, was also used by Scriabin. Schoenberg, however, has proceeded toward his goal more mathematically and scientifically.

The atonalists also avoid doubling any tone of a chord; in other words, each tone sounded must be different from the others—a four-tone chord must have four separate tones; one of them cannot be the same tone as another either in unison or in another octave. And better yet, each tone in a chord must have a dissonant tone to oppose it, a C matched by a C sharp or C flat; a G by a G sharp or a G flat, etc.

Construction of atonal music follows well-defined patterns. The rules of the system are as strict and rigid as any of those which limit the student of conventional harmony and counterpoint. If anything, the atonal rules are stricter. The fundamental basis of an atonal piece is known as the "row," or the succession of tones on which the composition is built. It is not accurate to speak of this row as a melody, or theme, for its succession of tones is subjected to such drastic alterations that it soon becomes unrecognizable to the average listener. The avowed purpose of the row is to establish and reveal the relations between the several tones used. Variations of the series are then employed to increase the number and variety of these relationships.

The first rule is that all the tones of the twelve-toned scale must be sounded before any of them is heard for the second time. This eliminates the possibility of any one tone becoming more important than the others. If C should be sounded twice, the listener might get the idea that the piece is written in the key of C. Once the complete row is announced, the piece continues in a manner similar to the variation form, and the row is subjected to a variety of manipulations and alterations. The intervals between tones may be made narrower or wider (shorter or longer skips and jumps); the intervals may remain the same, but the rhythm changed, elongated or contracted; some tones may be omitted and others added.

Two of the patterns for altering the twelve-tone row have descriptive names: the "mirror" and the "crab." The mirror is what its name implies, an inversion, or turning of the row upside down. When the skip from tone to tone represents an upward interval, the mirrored inversion presents the same interval in the opposite direction, or downwards the same number of scale degrees. In the "crab" pattern the row is sung or played as a crab travels, backwards. It starts with the last tone of the row, and then offers the whole series in reverse. The two patterns, the mirror and the crab, may also be combined, and the row played backwards *and* upside down, simultaneously. Atonal music might thus be described as music which may be played forwards, backwards, rightside up, or upside down.

As far as upside down is concerned, much of Bach's music is so constructed that it is highly effective when inverted in mirror fashion. I once tried an experiment in this direction with a player-piano roll of the second Prelude and Fugue from Volume I of the *Well-Tempered Clavichord*. Turning the roll so that the holes for the top notes would be at the bottom, and those for the low notes at the top, I placed the roll on the spool and turned the switch. The result was delightful. The rhythms, of course, remained the same; but the bass became the treble and the treble became the bass. Where the familiar themes leapt upward, the new ones plunged downhill. The entire work was so horizontally constructed that its outlines were as well defined in the inversion, and as melodically interesting, as they were in the accustomed position.

But to return to atonality. It is possible to grasp some idea of its underlying principles from verbal description, but the reader who wants to consider them visually and aurally will be interested in ex-

cerpts from one of Schoenberg's pieces. The following measures are taken from the fifth and last number of Opus 23, and they show some of the variations to which the twelve-tone row is subjected. The
piece is entitled *Walzer;* an almost ironic title, if you
try to waltz to the music.

There is, of course, no key signature, and the
twelve-tone row is set forth in the opening measure.
If you examine it carefully, you will find that no tone
in the upper part is repeated. Then look at the lower
part, and you will find that it, too, has twelve tones,
each of them different from the others:

In the following measures, the opening motive (the
first five tones of the upper part) is changed by hav-

ing its rhythm re-arranged. You will notice, also, that once more all twelve tones are sounded, and none repeated:

In a few measures the five-tone motive takes this form:

and is woven, horizontally, to the same motive arranged upside down and backwards:

Schoenberg's Walzer, *Op. 23, No. 5: Copyright, 1923, by Wilhelm Hansen. The excerpts have been printed by kind permission.*

A clear example of the mirror technique is found in a piece by an American composer, Gerald Strang, which is descriptively entitled *Mirrorrorrim*. This is not a strictly atonal work; it is cited merely to show how musical passages may be inverted:

Copyright, 1932, by Gerald Strang. Published by New Music.

At this point the layman is entitled to ask the pertinent question: how much of this is art, and how much mathematics? Assuming that art has an expressive function, that its reason for being is emotional as well as intellectual, exactly how expressive a medium is atonal music?

It is true that some highly expressive music has been created in the atonal pattern. The two operas of the late Alban Berg, *Wozzeck* and *Lulu*, are atonal works which are intense and dramatic, imaginative and colorful. *Lulu* is constructed entirely from a single twelve-tone row. It may be worth noting, however, that the theme of *Wozzeck* is that of a down-trodden, psychopathic soldier who stabs his unfaithful mistress and commits suicide by drowning, while *Lulu* offers a conception of womanhood which is expressed by the author of the libretto, Frank Wedekind, in a few lines from the Prologue:

> She was created to instigate harm,
> To lure, to seduce, to poison—
> To murder—without anyone's noticing.

It is doubtful that any system which limits itself so strictly and so arbitrarily to prescribed patterns can achieve unlimited expressive powers. Schoenberg himself has come to realize this, for he has publicly stated that when his system has become fully developed and the music-lover's ear has become accustomed to the new tonal relationships, consonances may be re-introduced with safety.

They will have to be included if atonal music is to have the flexibility and variety essential to any true work of art. Expressiveness depends so much on contrast that if the means of gaining contrast are denied the artist he cannot hope to convey his message. In the visual arts there are light and shade as well as colors; in prose and verse there is variety of mood and pace.

In tonal music there are a number of possible contrasts. Rhythmically, a composition may be played slowly or rapidly. Dynamically, it may be performed loudly or softly. Acoustically, the tonal range of voices and instruments affords a variety of pitch from the highest tones to the lowest. The mood-color of tonal music may be established, and altered, by the use of major and minor modes, while the sharpest contrasts of all are achieved by the interplay of consonance and dissonance.

Atonal music shares with tonal music only a few of these opportunities for contrast. It may be performed rapidly or slowly, loudly or softly. Its tones may be written in high registers or low. With these possibilities the similarity ends, for atonal music sacrifices the contrasts of major or minor, and of consonance and dissonance.

Aaron Copland has ventured a shrewd opinion on the future of atonal music. "Actually," he writes,[2] "it is rather difficult to foresee what the future has in store for most music written in the atonal idiom. Already it begins to sound surprisingly dated, hopelessly bound to the period of the twenties when it was first

[2] In *Our New Music*. New York: Whittlesey House, 1941.

played extensively. No doubt we are badly placed to judge it at present. But admitting our lack of sufficient perspective for judging it fairly, one can even now see certain inherent weaknesses; for whatever reasons, atonal music resembles itself too much. It creates a certain monotony of effect that severely limits its variety of expression. It has been said that the atonal system cannot produce folk songs or lullabies. But more serious is the fact that, being the expression of a highly refined and subtle musical culture, it has very little for a naïve but expanding musical culture such as is characteristic today of the United States (or the Soviet Union). This is not to deny its historical significance or its importance as an advanced outpost in the technicological field of musical experiment. But for a long time to come it is likely to be of interest principally to specialists and connoisseurs rather than to the generality of music lovers."

Of the various Schoenberg disciples, Alban Berg (1885–1935) was perhaps the most distinguished. Like Schoenberg, Berg was born in Vienna, and he died there before he had completely finished his second opera, *Lulu*. He first met Schoenberg in 1904, and it was because of the older musician's influence that he devoted himself exclusively to music.

In 1913 Schoenberg conducted a concert in Vienna

which presented Berg's first orchestral work, *Five Orchestral Songs to Picture-Postcard Texts by Peter Altenberg*. The performance caused one of the most notorious concert scandals that even Vienna had witnessed. The audience rioted so violently that the program had to be cut short.

The opera *Wozzeck* was completed in 1921 and produced at the State Opera in Berlin in 1924. Ten years later Berg finished a tentative version of *Lulu* in which the vocal parts were completely worked out but the orchestration merely sketched. Up to the time of his death he worked on the instrumentation, and finished all but the last two-thirds of the third act. He arranged a set of Five Symphonic Pieces from the score of *Lulu* which was performed in Berlin on November 30, 1934. Less than a month later he died of blood poisoning, and the scoring of the *Lulu's* last act was never completed by the composer. The first two acts were performed in 1937 at Zurich.

Lulu was not finished because the composer interrupted its composition during the Spring of 1935 to write a violin concerto. This work had been suggested to him by an American violinist, Louis Krasner. Berg was still considering the form the proposed work should take, when late in the Spring of 1935 he was saddened by the death of a young friend, Manon

Gropius. Working at feverish haste, he completed in a few months a violin concerto in the form of a requiem for Gropius. It proved to be his own requiem as well, for it was not until the April following the composer's death, that Krasner played it at the International Society for Contemporary Music Festival at Barcelona (1936).

Schoenberg took great pride and satisfaction in Berg, and never hesitated to pay tribute to what he regarded as his great genius. In 1930 Schoenberg remarked that he was proud that he had been able "to guide this great talent into the proper channels: towards the superb fulfillment of its individual potentialities, towards the greatest independence. But those qualities of mind and character which were indispensable for all this were innate in him and were in evidence at the very first lesson." [3]

More, perhaps, than any others of the atonalists, Schoenberg included, Berg actually used the atonal technique as a medium for a truly artistic, creative expression. It is true that the emotions and thoughts expressed by his music, particularly in his operas, are morbid and terrifying; but the music is exciting and stimulating, it gives the listener a valid emotional ex-

[3] Quoted in article on Berg by Willi Reich, in *The International Cyclopedia of Music and Musicians. Op. cit.*

(115)

perience. In addition, there are moments which are sensuous and lyrical.

Schoenberg's tribute to Alban Berg [4] contained an acknowledgment to another of his famous pupils, Anton von Webern, who was also a native of Vienna (born, Dec. 3, 1883): "Were not he [Berg], and our mutual friend and his fellow-pupil, Anton von Webern, the greatest credit to my influence as a teacher, and were not these two my support in times of greatest stress; for who could find anything better on this earth than their loyalty, steadfastness, and love?"

Von Webern's works include compositions for orchestra, chamber music and songs. He has regarded most literally the stipulation that atonalism calls for condensation and brevity, and as a result his pieces are brief to the point of monosyllabic terseness. Works of several movements require only a few minutes for performance; yet many people consider his music sensitive and perceptive.

Those who make a life study of atonalism are often scholars as well as musicians. Von Webern completed requirements for a Ph.D. degree at Vienna University, while another Schoenberg disciple and pupil, Egon Wellesz (Vienna, 1885), won a Ph.D. in 1908, and is a musicologist and music historian as well as

[4] *Ibid.*

a composer. Wellesz is an authority on Byzantine music, and the author of a two-volume work on *The New Instrumentation*. In addition to writing scholarly treatises, he is the composer of a long list of works: operas, ballets, orchestral compositions, and songs.

America has produced several atonalists. Prominent among them is Adolph Weiss (1891–) who studied with Schoenberg in Vienna. Schoenberg, however, says that Weiss is too independent a personality to be called his pupil. Weiss uses the twelve-tone row technique, liberally if not exclusively. In his Sonata for Flute and Viola he subjects his row to the mirror and crab alterations, and combines them simultaneously. His Piano Preludes provide excellent study material for the student of strict atonalism. In his *Kammersymphonie* Weiss builds the entire work on two intervals, and his *American Life* is constructed on a single interval.

Wallingford Riegger (Albany, Georgia, 1885) has become an avowed atonalist in his later works—*A Study in Sonority*, for ten violins or any multiple thereof; Three Canons for Woodwinds (1930); *Bacchanale* and *Evocation* (1931), and others more recent. Riegger has also become interested in writing music for the modern dance, and believes that it is

(117)

more valid and effective for the composer to write music after the choreography has been designed, than for the dancer to interpret a previously composed piece of music.

6

WRITING MUSIC IN TWO OR MORE
KEYS AT ONCE—POLYTONALITY

POLYTONALITY is the opposite of atonality. While the atonalists forego entirely the use of any definite key, the polytonalists write their music in two or more keys at the same time. Most of them, however, content themselves with two at a time.

A number of years ago, when radio was an infant, I was present at an event which gives a clear idea of what polytonality is, or might be. The Hungarian composer-pianist, Ernst von Dohnanyi, was to give a short recital of his own compositions on a local station in Philadelphia. That was before the day of networks, scripts written in advance, and split-second schedules. It was my duty to go to Philadelphia with Dohnanyi, see to it that he found his way to the studio, and look after him generally.

We had dinner together before the broadcast, and I suggested that inasmuch as I might be his announcer, wouldn't it help matters if I told something about the pieces he was to play? Accordingly, I took from my pocket an old envelope and jotted down what he told me. His first selection would be his Rhapsody in C minor, so I wrote: "Rhapsody, C minor." Next came his *Marche Humoresque*. This is a tricky piece which is built entirely over what is known as a "basso ostinato," or literally in English, an "obstinate bass" which refuses to change through the whole length of the piece. A little four-note figure in the left hand continues its way, constantly repeated and unchanged, from beginning to end.

I asked Dohnanyi what these four notes were, and he replied: "E flat, D, C, B flat." So I wrote on the envelope: "Marche Humoresque—E flat, D, C, B flat." When we arrived at the studio, I found that the resident announcer had no intention of letting any outsider do his announcing for him, so I hurriedly explained what I had planned to say about the pieces. I gave him the envelope, and told him about the Rhapsody in C minor and the bass figure in the *Marche Humoresque*. I showed him where I had written the names of the notes—E flat, D, C, and B flat, and then went to the piano and played them.

Soon it was time for the recital. The announcer introduced Dohnanyi with a rousing pep talk, and, consulting the envelope, said: "Mr. Dohnanyi's first piece is one he wrote himself; his Rhapsody in—er—" looking at the envelope again, "C minor." At the end of the Rhapsody, the announcer came to the microphone. "Mr. Dohnanyi will now play another piece he wrote himself: his *Marche Humoresque*, in—er—er," hurriedly looking at the envelope, "E flat, D, C, and B flat."

When the recital was over, Dohnanyi wiped his forehead. "Well," he said, "I like to be modern a little; but not so much as to write in *four* keys at once."

Unlike atonality, polytonality is not a system which requires detailed explanation, nor one which has a code of rules to govern its use. It is merely a practice of combining two or more tonalities, or keys, in any manner the composer wishes, and it is used in varying degrees by almost every present-day composer. There is, therefore, no group or cult of polytonalists, although some composers have made more extensive use of polytonal combinations than others.

In certain respects, polytonality is an extension and development of traditional devices which go back to the eighteenth century. It may be said to have its origin in a time-honored device known as "organ

point," sometimes called "pedal point." Organ point
consists of the holding or repetition of one tone, generally in the bass, while the other voices, or instrumental parts, continue their melodic and harmonic
progress, without regard to their relation to the sustained tone. An organ or pedal point generally begins
and ends at points where it harmonizes satisfactorily
with the other parts. The following example of organ
point is taken from the closing measures of a Bach
fugue: No. 2 in the first volume of the *Well-Tempered Clavichord:*

Bach made extensive use of organ point, generally
toward the close of his compositions, where it would
add to the summing-up effect which establishes the

idea of finality. The drone of bagpipes and the sustained tone of the musette are actually organ points.

As music has developed and its resources increased, composers have come to use more than one tone in organ point fashion. Often a whole chord of three or more tones is sustained, or repeated, while the other voices or instruments will sometimes pass into other keys before returning to a chord combination consonant with the multiple organ point. In this way polytonality is momentarily produced.

Still another forerunner of modern polytonality is a device which may be called polyharmony, and which is merely the sounding together of two different chords. Beethoven used polyharmony in the *Eroica* symphony by giving his hearers a dissonant chord and its resolution at the same time.

The difference between polyharmony and polytonality is easily understood by realizing that in polyharmony both chords may be spelled, or analyzed, in the same key. In the following combination:

the chord in the bass is the basic chord of C major. Although the upper chord could be considered the basic chord of G major, it is also one of the chords of C major, so that both chords belong to the key of C. Thus they produce polyharmony.

In the next combination, however:

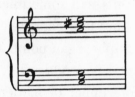

while the chord in the bass is again the fundamental chord of C major, the chord in the treble (upper part), with its C sharp, could not possibly be in that key, or in any other key to which the lower chord might belong. Therefore, no matter how the chords are analyzed, they are in different keys and polytonality results when they are sounded together.

In the chapter on dissonance we learned that Richard Strauss foreshadowed the coming of polytonality in the last bars of *Also sprach Zarathustra*. In that passage, composed in 1890, the basses sound the tones of the C major chord, and in the next measure the upper strings and wood winds play the B major chord. The two chords are not heard together, it is true, but the upper chord is sounded while the ear still retains the impression of the bass chord. Thus, the effect is distinctly polytonal, as though both were being sounded at the same time.

We have also learned that the impressionists inserted chords which are foreign to the underlying key of the passage in which they occur. Debussy's Prélude, *Canope,* contains chords in so many different keys that the ear gets the impression of several being played at once, even though each is sounded separately.

It is sometimes claimed that Igor Stravinsky was the first to make significant use of polytonality. This was in his ballet music for *Petrouchka,* composed in 1911. The so-called *Petrouchka* chord, used throughout the composition, represents two different keys, F sharp major and C major, sounded simultaneously:

Maurice Ravel explored the possibilities of polytonality with interesting results, yet he could never be accused of adopting any device merely to produce dissonant sounds. He was too much of a creative artist to use any pattern mechanically for its own sake, and when he employed polytonal combinations he did so because they enhanced his truly musical effects. Polytonality intensified the colors on his musical tone palette, and heightened the sensuous glamour of his scores.

As early as 1912, a year after Stravinsky produced *Petrouchka*, Ravel was experimenting with polytonality in his *Valses Nobles et Sentimentales*. In the opening measures of Valse No. 6, the upper wood winds play tones that are definitely in the key of D major. At the same time the upper strings and the horns are playing in B major, while the bass instruments play in C major. Thus we hear three tonalities at the same time: C, B, and D. In Valse No. 7, two keys are heard simultaneously: E major and F major.

Polytonality is often considered largely a French product, not because Ravel used it, but because it is so closely identified with the works of Darius Milhaud (1892–), and the so-called Parisian Group of Six, which included, besides Milhaud, five other French composers: Arthur Honegger (1892–), Francis Poulenc (1899–), Georges Auric (1899–), Germaine Tailleferre (1892–), and Louis Durey (1888–).

Les Six came into prominence shortly after the first World War, and became known as "Les Noveaux

Jeunes." For a literary spokesman, the members chose Jean Cocteau, and as musical sponsor, the eccentric Erik Satie. Under the name of "Les Six Française" the group achieved considerable notoriety and became the subject of many discussions and controversies. The six composers led a reaction against the "eloquence" of César Franck, the impressionism of Debussy, and what they termed the "scholasticism" of Vincent d'Indy. They adopted American jazz and imitated the music-hall style. After a few years, however, they lost their impetus and their identity as a group, and only two of them, Milhaud and Honegger, have retained the prominence they enjoyed as members of the radical *Les Six*.

Milhaud makes consistent use of polytonality. Perhaps this arises from, or at least explains, his kinship with the other members of *Les Six*, who, in reacting from Debussy's sensuousness, went headlong after brutal dissonance, as well as vivid colors and strong rhythms, turning their backs on anything hinting at sentiment. Milhaud had the conventional training at the Paris Conservatoire, under Gedalge, Widor, and d'Indy, and by the time he joined *Les Six* he had already composed a large amount of chamber music: four string quartets, two violin and piano sonatas, and

(127)

a sonata for piano, flute, oboe, and clarinet; orchestral music; a ballet; and incidental music to three dramas by Claudel.

The Sonata for flute, oboe, clarinet and piano, composed in 1918, is polytonal. In the first movement, the piano, oboe and clarinet start in F major, and the flute enters with a passage in C major. Later, when the piano shifts to F sharp major, the flute continues in C major.

When Milhaud associated with *Les Six,* he adopted jazz as wholeheartedly as any of his colleagues. In 1923 he completed his ballet, *La Création du Monde.* This work, based on a scenario by Blaise Cendars, deals with the creation of the world according to African legends. Jazz rhythms and blue notes permeate the entire score, all in various tonalities superimposed one on the other. Jazz subjects provide the basis for several fugues. It is interesting to observe that *La Création du Monde* was produced a year before George Gershwin composed his *Rhapsody in Blue.*

Milhaud's stage works include the ballet *Les Songes;* the operas: *Christoph Colomb* and *Le Pauvre Maledot;* and a number of others, including a group of so-called "minute-operas" which last no longer than eight minutes each. His list of orchestral and chamber-music works is likewise extended, and he has four compositions for solo piano and orchestra, and three for violin and orchestra. The piano concerto (1934) is distinctly polytonal. In the opening pages the orchestra plays in D major, and the solo piano in E major.

Notwithstanding his love of dissonance, which sometimes becomes downright cacophony, Milhaud is one of the most lyrically expressive of modern composers. His product is decidedly uneven, however, and he has adopted a bewildering variety of styles and idioms. His humor is often crude, particularly when he decides to set a florist's catalog to music for voice and orchestra.

Arthur Honegger became widely known to concert-goers through two works which achieved a vogue with symphony orchestras. The first of them, *Pacific 231*, depicts the powerful symmetry and dynamic energy of a great steam locomotive plunging through the night. The other, *Rugby*, deals with the swift energy and disciplined teamwork of English football. Honegger was a fellow-pupil of Milhaud at the Paris Conservatoire, but although Honegger was a prominent member of *Les Six*, he was not altogether in sympathy with its aims, particularly in its pursuit of jazz. In 1920 he announced that he did not profess the cult of the music hall and the street fair; on the contrary, he said, he sought the cult of chamber and symphonic music in their most serious and austere aspects.

Two of Honegger's outstanding works are based on Biblical subjects. One of them, *Le Roi David* (1921), is a symphonic psalm for chorus and orchestra, and the other, *Judith* (1925), is incidental music to a drama.

One of the most exquisite of Honegger's works is his *Pastorale d'Été*, for small orchestra, also available as a piano duet. In certain passages, particularly in the closing measures, this work is definitely polytonal, and in others it uses polyharmony by sounding simultaneously different chords in the single key of A major. The work is a splendid example of how delicately expressive, and how really beautiful, polytonality may become.

The Hungarian Béla Bartók (1881–) used polytonal harmonies more than thirty years ago. In many ways he has been as much a pioneer as Stravinsky or Schoenberg; he has experimented with involved and intricate rhythms, and at times he has departed so far from fixed tonality as to seem almost atonal. His music invariably avoids any semblance of sentimentality and his dissonances are sharp and biting.

It is not possible, however, to classify Bartók as a

polytonalist or an atonalist, for he has not consistently been either. He is more properly an intense nationalist, and the work he has accomplished in searching out and collecting Hungarian folk-music, in association with his fellow-countryman, Zoltán Kodály, has been of inestimable value in preserving excellent folk-melodies. These have shown the world what Hungarian music really is. Bartók has used this material in his own works, in highly modern fashion.

The American composer, Charles Ives (1874–), has made liberal use of polytonality, and in his setting of the *Sixty-Seventh Psalm*, for eight-part chorus of mixed voices, he affords a simple and clear example of writing in two keys at once. The treble voices (sopranos and altos) sing in C major, and the men's voices (tenors and basses) in G minor. In the score, each group has its own key signature:

GOD   BE   MER- CI -FUL UN –TO   US   *etc.*

Copyright, 1939, by Arrow Music Press, Inc.

Ives has been a truly rugged pioneer, and has become a unique figure among American composers.

For years he was known to only a few musicians, and was regarded seriously by still fewer of them. In 1939 his *Concord Sonata* for piano, which had been printed privately twenty years earlier, was played for the first time in New York's Town Hall by John Kirkpatrick. Lawrence Gilman, writing in the *Herald Tribune* proclaimed it "great music . . . indeed, the greatest music composed by an American, and the most deeply and essentially American in impulse and implication." Those were strong words, and while there were many who could not agree with Gilman, the pronouncement focussed attention on Ives and brought him a recognition at the age of sixty-four that he had neither sought nor gained before.

The remarkable feature of Ives's career is that he was experimenting with startling innovations when Schoenberg, Stravinsky, and other modernist composers were still writing in more or less conventional styles. He arrived at his own conclusions absolutely uninfluenced by the work of others.

Born in Danbury, Connecticut, he was the son of George E. Ives, who had been a bandmaster in Grant's army. The father was an adventurous spirit musically; he studied acoustics and experimented with quarter-tones. Charles Ives, the son, spent four years at Yale, where the conventional music training he received from Horatio Parker did not smother his pioneering spirit.

Instead of devoting all his time to music, he entered the insurance business in 1898, and later formed his own firm, in which he was active until 1930. Composing was kept as his pleasure and his hobby, and because he did not have to depend on it for his living he was able to write exactly as he pleased, without thought of money or fame. It may have been the musical impressions of his youth that shaped Ives's extraordinary music: the effect of two bands at opposite ends of the village green, each playing a different piece; reed organs out of tune; the music of country fiddlers; soldiers and bands marching, some out of step and trying to get in pace with their fellows.

In addition to publishing the *Concord Sonata* at his own expense in 1919, Ives issued in 1922 a volume of one hundred and fourteen songs, some of them simple and conventional, and some in the most advanced idiom imaginable. Recently a number of these songs have been reprinted in commercial editions. The composer has written for all mediums: orchestral works, chamber music, choral works, piano music, and songs.

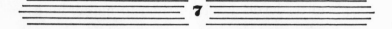

BACK TO BACH—NEO-CLASSICISM

An EDITORIAL writer for *Musical America* recently remarked: "We are now, it seems, in the 'neo' period of musical composition. The first thing for the aspiring composer to do today is to decide which 'neo' lodge he is going to join, and thereupon his cloth is cut for him and he wears the robes of his fellows. . . . If he wishes, the composer can be a 'neo-romantic,' or a 'neo-impressionist,' or a 'neo-classicist' or, I suppose, even a 'neo-neoist,' if he is a right smart fellow." [1]

According to the dictionary, the prefix "neo" indicates that the institution or style it qualifies is "new, recent, late," but Olin Downes, writing in the New York *Times*, wonders if "pseudo" would not be more accurate. He asks whether "the exponents of 'neo-

[1] "Mephisto's Musings," *Musical America*, Feb. 25, 1942.

(134)

classicism' don't really mean 'pseudo-classicism,' or just plain fake classicism, or the superficial imitation, in most unfortunate style, of the shell instead of the substance of the works of past masters."

If all the so-called neo-classic composers were mere imitators, Mr. Downes's indictment would be just, but a vast body of the important music from the twentieth century falls in the neo-classic category, and many of the leading composers of today belong in its camp. As a movement, neo-classicism is one of the significant manifestations of modern music.

Literally, the term means a *new* classicism, and it actually represents a turning back to the eighteenth century. Fundamentally, it is the twentieth century turning its back on the nineteenth century; the practical, machine age revolting against the *laissez faire* of the eighteen hundreds. The impulse of neo-classicism is the same as that which produced atonality, a reaction against romanticism and impressionism.

Unlike atonality, neo-classicism is not a tonal system. It makes use of any and all of the systems its composers choose. A neo-classic composition may be polytonal or atonal, it may make use of the dissonances of Debussy or Ravel, or it may be somewhat conventional. Neo-classicism is a matter of form and spirit, rather than one requiring fixed patterns of tonal combinations. Hence, we do not speak of neo-classic chords or harmonies, as we speak of atonal, or polytonal passages.

We have already learned how the nineteenth century romanticists, in reacting from the formalism of the classic composers, became concerned more with the emotional content of their music than with its outer form. The neo-classic composers have reversed the process; now that romanticism has had its) day, they, in turn, seem more concerned with perfection of form than with the content or poetic significance of their music. Thus we find the Russian Prokofieff composing a *Classical Symphony*, others writing *Concerti Grossi*, all in eighteenth century forms. The difference between the twentieth and eighteenth century works is that modern composers, although they are writing in old forms, are allowing themselves the dissonant technique of the present day, and the privilege of disregarding the traditional rules of strict harmony and counterpoint.

Marion Bauer, in her article on "Neo-Classicism" in the *International Cyclopedia of Music and Musicians*,[2] describes the neo-classic composers as "more impersonal, intellectual and abstract than personal, emotional, and programmatic. The Twentieth

[2] Oscar Thompson (editor). New York: Dodd, Mead & Co.

Century," she writes, "in its fear of being regarded as over-sentimental and romantic, sought complete emancipation from the graphic, the literary, the philosophical, and the emotional in music."

We find, then, that the neo-classic composers aim at simplification of their music. Like the atonalists, they eliminate what they consider non-essential, and they condense their material as much as possible. Many neo-classic works are composed for small ensembles, and reacting from the enormous, complex orchestrations of Berlioz, Wagner and Richard Strauss, they are often scored for chamber orchestra.

It is not altogether accurate to say that neo-classicism is an immediate reaction against romanticism, that the cycle has been a simple three-part pattern of classicism, romanticism, new-classicism. Several intermediary steps intervened between romanticism and neo-classicism, and the most important of them is sometimes called primitivism, or what might be termed a downright barbarism in music. This represented a reversion almost to the cave man, and involved primitive rites and a tonal fury that blasted the ears of concert-goers. Primitivism undoubtedly had its background in the political, social, and economic upheavals of the first two decades of the century, the years when unrest was first appearing, and when the World War No. 1 was disrupting Europe's complacency.

The passing from primitivism to neo-classicism is best understood through the career of Igor Stravinsky, the Russian-born composer who has been a leader in the back-to-the-classics movement. Some critics accuse Stravinsky of an inconsistent adoption of so many different styles that he has become a musical hybrid; but whatever anyone may think of his later works, his career represents a definite series of developments which are characteristic of the course modern music has taken in the last quarter-century.

Stravinsky was born in Oranienbaum, Russia, June 17, 1882. His father was a bass singer at the Imperial Opera, and although Igor was not a child prodigy, he was reared in a musical atmosphere, and as a youth tried his hand at composing. When he was nineteen, he met Rimsky-Korsakoff, who suggested that he study with one of his own pupils. Then, when Stravinsky was sufficiently prepared, Rimsky-Korsakoff accepted him as a private pupil, in 1907.

Stravinsky's early works were thoroughly academic and conventional. His first symphony, composed in 1905–07, is Brahmsian in style, and shows no contemporary influences. A suite of songs for mezzosoprano and orchestra, however, contains elements of impressionism. These were composed in 1908 when Stravinsky had commenced his studies with Rimsky-Korsakoff. In the same year he composed a symphonic poem, *Fireworks,* to celebrate the marriage of Rimsky-Korsakoff's daughter. Four days after the ceremony, Rimsky-Korsakoff died, and Stravinsky composed a memorial, *Chant funèbre.*

Stravinsky was inactive for a short period after Rimsky's death, but a new stimulus appeared in the person of Sergei Diaghileff, who was organizing his *Ballet Russe* in Paris. It was Diaghileff, and the Russian ballet, who were directly responsible for Stravinsky's most important works. Early in 1909 Stravinsky's *Fantastic Scherzo* was performed in St. Petersburg, and Diaghileff was impressed with the way in which Stravinsky wrote for orchestra. He commissioned Stravinsky to orchestrate two Chopin pieces, a Nocturne and a Valse, for use in the ballet, *Les Sylphides.* Stravinsky laid aside an opera he had started, *Les Rossignol,* and made the orchestration for Diaghileff. Then he returned to his work on the opera.

He had no more than finished the first act when Diaghileff called on him once more, this time with a commission for an original work: a ballet based on a Russian fairy-tale, *The Fire Bird.* Stravinsky went to work immediately and completed the score in May of 1910, for production in Paris the following month.

With the *Fire Bird* music a new Stravinsky appeared, a true disciple of Rimsky-Korsakoff and an exponent of the Russian national school. The orchestra he used was the orchestra of *Scheherazade,* and the oriental elements of Rimsky's style were amplified and brought up-to-date in brilliant fashion. It was not Rimsky-Korsakoff, nor his shade, however, who composed the *Fire Bird;* in spite of the influences it showed, the music belonged distinctively to Stravinsky, and the *Fire Bird* was an acknowledged masterpiece.

Diaghileff showed his pleasure by commissioning another ballet the following year. This was *Petrouchka,* which was first produced at Paris in June, 1911. This music originated with an instrumental *Konzertstück* which Stravinsky had sketched for piano and orchestra. As the score developed, the piano and the orchestra were given a dialogue, each answering and imitating the other, which brought to the composer's imagination the vision of a mischievous, aggravating puppet, the counterpart of *Petrouchka,* who was the hero of an ancient Russian marionette show, a Muscovite *Punch and Judy.*

As a ballet, *Petrouchka* was immediately successful, but its musical significance was far greater than people realized at first. The music marked a transition in Stravinsky's style, from the fantasy of the *Fire Bird* to realism. The *Fire Bird* had a generous share of sustained, flowing melody, even though it was far more advanced harmonically than the works of Stravinsky's teacher, Rimsky-Korsakoff. *Petrouchka* is episodic, loosely constructed, and highly dissonant. If the *Fire Bird* represents the bridge between the nineteenth and twentieth centuries, *Petrouchka* is pure twentieth; at least, early twentieth century.

Most important of all, however, was the introduction of polytonality, for by his use of the *Petrouchka* chord, Stravinsky became a pioneer in using two keys at the same time. It may have been an accident; Stravinsky may have been amused by playing on the white keys with his right hand and on the black keys with his left, but at any rate the vogue of polytonality dates from the appearance of the *Petrouchka* chord.

The realism of *Petrouchka* led to the primitivism of the next ballet Stravinsky composed for Diaghileff, *Le Sacre du Printemps*, the *Rite of Spring*. When this work was produced in Paris, May 29, 1913, it aroused such fury that the audience rioted. The music was so dissonant, so bewildering, that the world was faced "with the alternative either to reject this music as a freakish exhibition of an unbalanced young man, or accept it as a revolutionary innovation." [3]

It is important to consider *Le Sacre* carefully for the moment, for it represents a point in Stravinsky's career which is soon to be followed by a turn in the opposite direction, from the height of complexity to the utmost simplicity. *Le Sacre* is scored for an orchestra of tremendous size, and it employs crashing chords which were almost unbelievable to the ears of pre-War concert-goers. Anyone who knew Stravinsky's background, however, and was familiar with the *Fire Bird* and *Petrouchka,* was aware that *Le Sacre* could not be a haphazard product, but that its composer was fully conscious of what he was doing, and was accomplishing his purpose with a masterful, though grim and almost diabolical, grasp of his medium and his materials.

Le Sacre du Printemps deals with the sacrificial customs of primitive peoples, barbaric, brutal pagan rites, and it is not to be expected that a composer like Stravinsky would have depicted primitive man with the cloying sweetness of conventional harmonies. Stravinsky claims that he would have written this sort of music even if he had not been writing it for the

[3] Nicolas Slonimsky in his article on Stravinsky in *The International Cyclopedia of Music and Musicians. Op. cit.*

ballet. He says that he conceived it first as absolute music, entirely apart from any plot, and that its rough, uncouth themes themselves suggested to his mind the earth worship of primitive man. Thus, the idea for the ballet came from the music; not the music from the plot of the ballet.

This statement is important in showing that Stravinsky's primitivism was a definite stage in his musical development. First had come the fantasy of the *Fire Bird,* the opulence of the Russian-Oriental school; then, the hard realism of *Petrouchka;* and, third, the barbaric primitivism of *Le Sacre.* The world might well wonder what the next step would be, but it was not for another ten years that it found out, and by that time a colossal war had shaken the world.

Just before the war, Stravinsky passed through a period during which he was absorbed in Russian folklore; and, again using the utmost in performing resources, he composed *Les Noces,* a grandiose work for solo voices, chorus, four pianos, and seventeen percussion instruments. The composition of the "choreographic Russian scenes" which comprised *Les Noces* took altogether seven years, for the war interrupted its composition. *Les Noces* has something of the primitive quality of *Le Sacre,* but its primal urge is apparent through the roistering of peasants, rather than through the barbaric earth-worship of pre-historic man.

While *Les Noces* was still unfinished, Stravinsky, still absorbed in Russian folk-lore, set to music a Russian tale about a deserting soldier and the devil. This *Histoire du Soldat*, unlike *Le Sacre* or *Les Noces*, is most economical in its use of theatrical and musical resources. It is theatre music which requires only a few actors, and a small ensemble of seven instruments.

Following the idea of writing for limited combinations, Stravinsky continued to write for small groups, even when he became interested in American jazz, and composed his *Ragtime* for eleven instruments. He wrote a little suite of pieces for clarinet, without accompaniment, and in 1919 made a re-orchestration of the *Fire Bird* music, more restrained and less colorful than the original, and scored for a smaller orchestra.

All these intermediary ventures were a preliminary to the actual turning point, which came when Stravinsky composed his *Pulcinella* ballet, produced in Paris May 15, 1920. This work was based entirely on the music of the early eighteenth century composer, Pergolesi, and although Stravinsky was by no means a mere arranger in adapting this music, he retained the exact spirit of Pergolesi's style, and kept his own score chastely simple. There was no attempt at modernization.

Pulcinella marked the beginning of Stravinsky's neo-classic period. By adhering to the classicism of Pergolesi's eighteenth century style, Stravinsky had so imbued himself with its spirit that he was ready to adapt it to original compositions of his own invention. Thus he has completed in his own creative career a cycle which passed from late-romanticism, through realism and primitivism, to a pure objectivism which is marked by a detached viewpoint and a formalism that reverts to Bach and Handel. Stravinsky finished the movement that the Russian nationalists began fifty years before him, in the eighteen seventies. They wanted to rid music of the strangle hold of German romanticism, and Stravinsky finished the job completely and effectively.

In 1923 Stravinsky offered his first original work in the pure neo-classic manner, his Octet for Wind Instruments. In writing it he imposed upon himself the limitations that surrounded the early masters. He kept to the forms and the patterns of the classicists, and even though he modernized his structure by

using present-day devices, polytonality and dissonance, he soft-pedalled the radical elements that had
marked his earlier works.

Other Stravinsky works in the neo-classic manner
are the *Symphony of Psalms*, (1930) for chorus, an
opera-oratorio, *Oedipus Rex* (1927), and the ballet,
Apollon Musagètes (1927). Another ballet, *Le Baiser
de la Fée* (1928) is based on Tschaikowsky themes,
and *Card Party* (1936), a ballet in three deals, describes a game of poker. Since taking up his residence
in America, Stravinsky has paid tribute to his adopted
country by making a new orchestration of *The Star
Spangled Banner*.

Condensation of material is a feature of neo-
classicism, just as it is of atonality. In neo-classicism,
however, this condensation is adopted as a step
towards simplification. Stravinsky once explained the
need for brevity by pointing out the essential differences between eighteenth- and twentieth-century
classicism. "For a Mozart," he wrote,[4] "the invention
of the theme, or of the themes, represented . . . the
maximum effort; all the rest was made up in great
part of a certain formalism, or at least technical skill
had the upper hand over creative fantasy. . . . With

[4] As quoted by Lawrence Gilman in Program Notes for the
Philadelphia Orchestra Concerts, Jan. 5, 1932.

the developments of the theme, the repetitions, refrains, and necessary 'cadenze,' the half-hour was soon reached.

"But now that in a scholastic sense this development of the theme no longer exists, and still less repetitions, . . . proportions have changed, and a concerto of fifteen minutes is already a monumental work. Naturally it would be easy to lengthen the duration, but what would be added would be nothing but padding, inert matter, sound, but not music."

In reverting to the patterns of the eighteenth century, as well as to its ideals and spirit, the neo-classicists naturally turn to the contrapuntal style of Bach and Handel; to horizontal weaving of parts and voices, and the forms of the canon and fugue. Where, however, the eighteenth century masters limited themselves largely to consonant counterpoint, the modern classicists allow themselves far more latitude. They are not required to shape the themes of their canons and fugues so that each part, or voice, will "make harmony" with the others. Thus the characteristic counterpoint of the twentieth century is dissonant counterpoint; the structures of fugues are identical with those of a couple of centuries ago, but their acrid dissonances and biting combinations of tones belong to our time.

The *Classical Symphony* of Serge Prokofieff is an outstanding product of the neo-classic movement, and is significant in being the work of a composer who started his career as a musical radical. Prokofieff is a Russian, born April 23, 1891, nine years later than Stravinsky. Like Stravinsky, Prokofieff studied for a time with Rimsky-Korsakoff. His early works were highly original, and were marked by aggressive rhythms and bold harmonies. They had a driving dynamic power which was all the more pronounced when tinged with Prokofieff's love for the grotesque. They used almost every modern device except atonality, which appears in only one Prokofieff work, the cantata, *Seven, They Are Seven*. The *Classical Symphony* was composed in 1917, antedating Stravinsky's neo-classic Octet by six years, and the *Pulcinella* suite by one year. Prokofieff, then, was a neo-classicist before Stravinsky, but in his later works he has not followed the movement as closely as Stravinsky has.

The *Classical Symphony* is concise, and written in four short movements according to the eighteenth-century pattern, substituting a gavotte for the customary minuet as the dance movement. Prokofieff explained that his idea in writing the symphony was "to catch the spirit of Mozart, and to put down that which, if he were living now, Mozart might put into his scores." Hence, the music is marked by melodies which Mozart might conceivably have written, but colored with harmonic modernisms and sophistications which would have been puzzling to Mozart living in the eighteenth century. They might have pleased him, however, if he had been living in 1917.

After the war the ways of Stravinsky and Prokofieff became widely separated, principally because Stravinsky had no sympathy with the Russian Revolution and the Soviet, while Prokofieff has kept in touch with Russia, and has lent his talents to the Communist cause. In 1937 he wrote a grandiose cantata, for the twentieth anniversary of the October Revolution, to a text made from the speeches of Lenin, Stalin and Marx.

Following the production of his opera, *The Love for Three Oranges* (in Chicago, 1921), Prokofieff followed Stravinsky's example by writing ballets for Diaghileff. The first, *Buffoon,* was produced in Paris in 1921. Then came *Le Pas d'Acier* (*The Age of Steel*) in 1927, and *L'enfant prodigue* in 1929. He composed also a number of purely instrumental works: five piano concertos, two violin concertos, a 'cello concerto, and four symphonies, of which the *Classical Symphony* was the first.

Whatever it may indicate, the Soviet period of

Prokofieff's works has brought a lyric quality to his music which has overshadowed the grotesque touches that were so prominent in his early compositions. He has kept, however, the childlike sense of humor so delightfully apparent in the musical fairy-tale for children, *Peter and the Wolf*. In this score each character is represented by an instrument in the orchestra: the Wolf by the French horns, Peter's grandfather by the bassoon, etc.

Dmitri Shostakovich, born in Russia in 1906, ranks with Stravinsky and Prokofieff as one of the three most important composers Russia has produced in modern times. Aside from his undoubted talent, Shostakovich is interesting as an example of a creative artist adapting himself to political and social changes, and to the tastes of a mass public.

He composed his first symphony when he was nineteen, and through its performance a year later he attracted immediate attention. Here was a work which had ingenious melodies and novel rhythms; it was modern enough to be interesting, and academic enough to be agreeable and understood. In a way it was neo-classic, for it was direct and to the point, with a structural design that was easily followed.

A year later Shostakovich presented his second symphony, written for the tenth anniversary of the

Soviet Republic. This did not meet with the success of the first symphony. Next, the composer wrote an opera, *The Nose,* which satirized an important government official. In its score Shostakovich became complex, and used atonal patterns. The opera was produced at Leningrad in 1930, and was assailed by the Russian Association of Proletarian Composers as a product of "bourgeois decadence."

The Third Symphony, like the second, had political significance. Modeled after the Ninth Symphony of Beethoven, it ended with a choral movement in the form of a Mayday Hymn. This symphony was followed by two more ballets, both of them satirical, with indictments of non-Soviet peoples. Then came a most significant work, a second opera, *Lady Macbeth of the District of Mzensk.* In spite of a highly suggestive interlude, which was eliminated from Russian productions of the opera, *Lady Macbeth* enjoyed a vogue in Russia and in other countries. Official indictment, however, in the form of an article in *Pravda,* condemned the work as theatrically vulgar and "musically formalistic."

This article was followed by another, in the same periodical, which attacked a Shostakovich ballet, *The Limpid Stream,* as a frivolous and over-simplified essay on the subject of collective farming. It looked as though official disfavor would bring an end to Shostakovich's brilliant career. To prevent this, the young composer accomplished a complete change of creative style, and was genius enough to do it successfully. He withdrew a fourth symphony, and started writing a fifth, which was performed late in 1937, and achieved tremendous success. Shostakovich again became the favorite composer of the Russian people, and the musical spokesman for the Soviet government.

During the summer of 1942 (July 19), the NBC Symphony Orchestra, under Toscanini, gave the first American performance to Shostakovitch's Seventh Symphony. This was one of the first major works to be inspired by the second World War, and it was composed, for the most part, near one of the fighting fronts. The composer began it in June, 1941, and wrote much of the score in Leningrad while he was engaged in watching for fires and in other defense activities of the besieged city.

Many difficulties stood in the way of sending a copy of the score to America. It was photographed on microfilm, and the tiny roll of film was sent from Russia in April, 1942. It was carried by plane, automobile, and again by plane, and finally reached New

York early in June. Toscanini immediately arranged for its performance the following month.

The symphony is dedicated "to our struggle against Fascism, to our future victory, to my native city, Leningrad." It is a lengthy work; the American première ran about an hour and a quarter, and critical opinion agreed upon the sincerity of the symphony and the imposing effect of the climaxes, but observed that it was marred by unevenness of outline, resulting perhaps from the circumstances of its composition. There could hardly have been opportunity, under the conditions, for the composer to sift and weigh the value of his material, and subject it to self-criticism.

The neo-classic movement has touched composers of widely separated styles and ideals. In Spain, we find Manuel de Falla composing a Harpsichord Concerto (1923–26), for harpsichord (or piano) and flute, oboe, clarinet, violin, and 'cello. De Falla is steeped in the Spanish tradition, and through his own individuality has brought a fusion of his nation's past and present.

In Italy, Alfredo Casella was at one time violently assailed for his modernism, and his *Elegia Eroica*, dedicated to the war dead, provoked a riot when it was performed at Rome in 1917. Casella worked out a polytonal style which was lacking in all the chromaticisms of the romanticists. More recently his Concerto for String Quartet, composed in 1923–24, reverted to an Italian classicism, even though it employed an extended tonal system. In 1926 he followed the example of Stravinsky's *Pulcinella*, by writing a work for piano and orchestra called *Scarlattiana*, based on themes of Scarlatti.

The Swiss-American Ernest Bloch (1880–) has composed a Concerto Grosso for strings and piano obbligato, which offers new ideas in old patterns; while another American, Albert Stoessel (1894–), has to his credit a Concerto Grosso, for the same combination of instruments, adhering to the old forms, but employing dissonant counterpoint. Three of these composers, de Falla, Casella, and Bloch have already been mentioned for their impressionist tendencies.

The two Americans most closely identified with neo-classicism are Walter Piston (1894–) and Roger Sessions (1896–). In spite of his advanced harmonic combinations, Piston is always direct and to the point; he respects convention in the formal design of his structure, and he is exceedingly fond of imitative counterpoint, and the canon and fugue of the eighteenth century. His music for the ballet,

The Incredible Flutist, is delightful in its simplicity, while the first movement of his Concerto for Orchestra is close to the spirit of the old Concerto Grosso. Piston is a native of Maine, born in 1894. At present he is head of the music department at Harvard University.

Sessions has acknowledged Stravinsky's influence, but he insists that he does not belong to any "school" or limited group of stylists. In 1927 he announced: "I reject any kind of dogma or platform. I am not trying to write 'modern,' 'American,' or 'neo-classic' music. I am seeking always and only the coherent and living expression of my musical ideas." [5] In spite of this disclaimer, there is in Sessions' mature work an orthodox feeling for form; his String Quartet most certainly labels him as a composer with the ideals of a classicist. He is by nature a perfectionist, which is perhaps responsible for his relatively small number of works. In the 1927 statement he declared: "I dislike rhetoric, overemphasis, vulgarity, but at the same time believe that perfection in art consists in a sort of equilibrium which can be neither defined nor counterfeited."

In his Three Chorales for Organ and in his Piano Sonata, Sessions shows his love for perfection in de-

---

[5] Quoted by Nicolas Slonimsky in *American Composers on American Music.* Stanford University Press, 1933.

sign and structure, and sometimes the manner in which he expresses his ideas is more significant than the ideas themselves. He has also three symphonies, a Concerto for Violin and Orchestra, three dirges for orchestra, and several other works which have had successful performances. Like Piston, he is a teacher of composition, and is associated with the music department of Princeton University.

One of the most frequently heard native composers is Roy Harris, born in Oklahoma, February 12, 1898. Harris is one of the most picturesque and colorful figures among our creative musicians. It is not easy to classify him for he does not fit neatly into any grouping. He is polytonal whenever he finds that combined tonalities answer his purpose; he is rarely, if ever, atonal; his intense Americanism, with its racy flavor of the Southwest, gives his work a highly nationalistic character. He is, however, very much the neo-classicist in his attempt to adapt old forms to present-day needs.

The remarkable feature of the Harris vogue is that the composer makes no compromise whatever with the conservative elements in his audiences. He never tries to write music that will be easy for traditionally conditioned ears to listen to; much of his work is difficult and disconcerting at first hearing. His dissonances are uncompromising and caustic, and his structure is involved and complex in spite of his neo-classic leanings.

Recently Harris has been composing music for performance by young people. His song, *Freedom's Land,* a setting of a poem by Archibald MacLeish, is being sung in schools throughout the country, and by troops in Army camps. His Concerto for Piano and Symphonic Band had its first performance by the University of Michigan Concert Band, with Johana Harris, the composer's wife, playing the solo part. Harris feels that the youth of today is perfectly at home in an atmosphere of modern rhythms, harmony and form, so he makes no concessions when he writes for young performers.

Behind all of Harris's works there is an idealism and a philosophy which motivate his underlying principles and crystallize his thought. The explanation he advanced for his first symphony is characteristic. In its three movements, he said, he tried first "to capture the mood of adventure and physical exuberance"; then to show "the pathos which seems to underlie all human existence"; and finally, to catch "the mood of a positive will to power and action."

His long list of works includes four symphonies, an orchestral suite, a piano sonata, several string quartets, a sextet, a *Symphony for Voices,* and many others.

8

WORKADAY MUSIC FOR EVERY-DAY

USE—GEBRAUCHSMUSIK

CLOSELY ALLIED with neo-classicism, principally because it also tends to simplify music, is *Gebrauchsmusik,* tagged with a German label since it originated in the post-War Germany of the 1920's. Literally translated, the term means "music for use," and that is exactly what it is.

About fifteen years ago, a number of composers became aware of the fact that their audience of educated music lovers was pitifully small, and that they were completely out of touch with the vast potential audience of young people and of older persons who were not in the habit of going to concerts. Perhaps the radio and sound pictures had something to do with it, but at any rate a few musicians felt that if they could write music which would be played in other places than the concert halls and grand-opera houses, they would have a wider market for their product.

Consequently, they decided to compose what might be termed practical, or workaday, music, which would either be adapted to the needs of musical amateurs, or written for some specific purpose outside the accepted channels of symphony orchestras or opera companies. The *Gebrauchsmusik* movement has taken two directions: the first, developing music for amateurs to perform—operettas and cantatas for school children, instrumental pieces for school and college orchestras, and works in which the audience participates by singing some of the choruses and songs. The other type of *Gebrauchsmusik* is for performance by professionals, but intended for a wide audience: incidental music for sound pictures and plays and for radio, light operas which have popular appeal, and music which has political and social significance in a changing world.

It is generally believed that the *Gebrauchsmusik* movement had its impetus from the German composer, Paul Hindemith, in the years around 1927. Hindemith, born in 1895 at Hanau, near Frankfort, is a composer who started his career with a thoroughly practical and wide experience. At the age of thirteen he had mastered the violin, and played widely in orchestras at motion picture houses, musical comedy theatres, in dance bands, and, finally, in symphony orchestras. He studied at Hoch's Conservatory in Frankfort, and from 1915 to 1923 was concert-master at the Frankfort Opera. He also founded a string quartet. Finally he became professor at the Hochschule in Berlin, where he remained until the displeasure of the Third Reich caused him to make his home in the United States.

As a composer, Hindemith showed from the start his practical experience as an orchestral musician, as well as a sense of humor which could be either playful or ironical. At first his music reflected the influence of such composers as Brahms and Max Reger, but he eventually put aside romantic tendencies and turned to a style closely allied to neo-classicism, reflecting the detached, impersonal point of view which he had consciously adopted.

Hindemith's works for the accustomed audience of music lovers cover a wide range, for he has been prolific. There are several operas, of which *Mathis der Maler* is the best known; an orchestral symphony from the same opera; a Concerto for Orchestra; five works for chamber orchestra which he calls *Kammermusik*; four string quartets; two string trios; a number of sonatas for various instruments and combinations; three sonatas and a suite for piano, as well as a considerable list of piano pieces, songs, and choral works. Although Hindemith has at times departed so far from mixed tonalities as to omit key signatures, he has never been an actual atonalist. In recent years his feeling for tonality has re-asserted itself, and whatever he writes nowadays has a distinct tonal center.

In 1927 Hindemith summarized his attitude regarding practical uses for music in the following words: [1] "It is to be regretted that in general so little relationship exists today between the producers and the consumers of music. A composer should write today only if he knows for what purpose he is writing. The days of composing for the sake of composing are perhaps gone forever. On the other hand, the demand for music is so great that composer and consumer ought most emphatically to come at last to an understanding."

The works that Hindemith has composed for his new audience cover a wide field. First there were a number of pieces for mechanical instruments; then came music to accompany a motion picture film, *Felix the Cat*, to be played by a mechanical organ. These works are still in manuscript, but in 1927 Hindemith published a number of pieces for amateurs: *Spielmusik* (*Music to Play*) for strings, flutes, and oboes; a group

---

[1] Quoted by Willi Reich in an article on Hindemith in the *Musical Quarterly*, October, 1931.

of Songs for Singing Groups; and an educational work for violin ensembles. After these, in later years, came a variety of music to sing or play, designed for use by amateurs or music lovers. Some of them call for audience participation through community singing. *Let's Build a Town*, composed in 1931, is a play with music for children.

Motion pictures naturally provided an attractive vehicle for the kind of music Hindemith wanted to write, and in his work at the Hochschule in Berlin he conducted a Film-Music Studio. Here he put his pupils to work studying the mechanical processes of film production. They learned to synchronize musical measures with sections of film, and composed music to old films, cut and fitted for the purpose.

Kurt Weill is another German exponent of *Gebrauchsmusik*. Born in Dessau, 1900, he set himself the task of developing a new type of musical play. His first important experiment in this direction was called *Die Dreigroschenoper* (*The Three-Penny Opera*), which took for its pattern Gay's famous *Beggar's Opera*. In recent years he has lived in America, where he has composed incidental music for plays as well as scores for sound pictures and several musical comedies. In 1933 his two-act operetta, *Der Jasager*,

intended for performance for young people, was produced by the Music School of the Henry Street Settlement in New York. He composed incidental music for
Max Reinhardt's New York production of Franz Wer-
fel's play, *The Eternal Road,* and in 1936 he supplied
a musical background for Paul Green's *Johnny John-
son.* He collaborated with Maxwell Anderson in writing the musical comedy which starred Walter Huston,
Knickerbocker Holiday (1938), and he composed the
score for the New York World's Fair transportation
pageant, *Railroads on Parade* (1939–40). For radio,
he wrote the music for Maxwell Anderson's "Ballad
History," *Magna Charta,* performed on the Columbia
network in 1940.

Ernst Křenek, born in Vienna, 1900, and now living in the United States, has been known both as
a neo-classicist and as an atonalist, having adopted
Schoenberg's twelve-tone technique and altered it to
suit his own purposes. He achieved his greatest fame,
however, by a work which was closely allied with the
Gebrauchsmusik movement, an opera which incorporated American jazz patterns, entitled *Jonny spielt
auf.* This work was rejected by several leading theatres
in Germany, but was finally produced at Leipzig in
1927. It scored such a tremendous success that it was

eventually performed in more than one hundred cities and translated into eighteen languages. In 1929 it was produced at the Metropolitan in New York.

Both Weill and Křenek have succeeded in giving large audiences an art-music they can comprehend. In their stage works they substituted for the high-flown aria, songs in the musical comedy manner, some of them in the jazz vein. On the whole, they have succeeded in producing an art product which has popular appeal, and which successfully avoids being "arty," or over-precious.

Marc Blitzstein, born in Philadelphia in 1905, has shown the influence of Kurt Weill by developing a type of stage entertainment which may conceivably develop into an indigenous form of opera. He employs a type of performer who might be termed a singing-actor rather than an acting-singer, and he provides his characters with dialogue and lyrics of his own writing which are convincing and realistic. In 1937 Blitzstein's satiric light-opera, *The Cradle Will Rock*, was produced at the Mercury Theatre in New York, and was so successful that it had a run of several months. This was followed by a similar work, *No for an Answer*, as well as a half-hour radio opera, *I've Got the Tune*.

Blitzstein indoctrinates his works with left-wing theories which lend them the function of class-struggle propaganda. This limits their appeal, but it provides them a purpose which is sincere and direct.

Many other American composers have interested themselves in the new market for their music, and have come to realize that the millions of children who are nowadays receiving instrumental as well as vocal training in the schools, need good music written especially for them. Thus we find such composers as Douglas Moore (1893–) composing an operetta for amateur and school groups, *The Headless Horseman,* first produced in Bronxville, New York, in 1937.

High-school orchestras are a particularly tempting market, for there are thousands of them, and since they are made up of twentieth-century youngsters, they are interested in twentieth-century music.

The sound-pictures, too, have need for serious composers as well as for the tunesmiths who write songs for the so-called "musicals" and "revues." Producers have found that musical background is essential for drama, to blend and tie together moods and atmosphere, and to establish continuity and contrast between episodes and scenes. Werner Janssen, George Antheil, Louis Gruenberg, are but a few of the prominent American composers whom Hollywood has called upon for originally composed scores to accompany films.

Radio has proved a fertile field for experiment. Many of its presentations, particularly in the operatic field, have been adaptations of stage works, but the leading networks have encouraged, through commissions and prize contests, the writing of operas and operettas primarily intended for radio presentation. Among them have been Gian-Carlo Menotti's *The Old Maid and the Thief* (NBC, 1939); Louis Gruenberg's *Green Mansions* (CBS, 1936); Vittorio Giannini's *Beauty and the Beast* (CBS, 1938) and *Blennerhassett* (CBS, 1939); and Randall Thompson's *Solomon and Balkis* (CBS, 1942). In addition, dozens of instrumental works have been composed with radio requirements in mind, as well as background scores for radio dramas.

The music these men have composed for these twentieth-century media has generally been thoroughly contemporary in spirit, and has made liberal use of the new idioms that have been developed.

Aaron Copland, born in Brooklyn, New York, in 1900, has been a prominent leader among American composers in the movement to compose art-works which are practical for performance by a wider circle than professional musicians, or are designed for the constantly increasing audience of listeners outside the concert halls—on the radio, in motion picture houses, and in the theatre. In his recent book, *Our New Music,*[2] Copland gives an interesting account of himself and of his aims. In the chapter, *Composer from Brooklyn,* he explains: "During these years [1930–1935] I began to feel an increasing dissatisfaction with the relations of the music-loving public and the living composer. The old 'special public' of the modern music concerts had fallen away, and the conventional concert public continued apathetic or indifferent to anything but the established classics. It seemed to me that we composers were in danger of working in a vacuum. Moreover, an entirely new public for music had grown up around the radio and phonograph. It made no sense to ignore them and to continue writing as if they did not exist. I felt it was worth the effort to see if I couldn't say what I had to say in the simplest possible terms."

Before he came to this decision, Copland had already established himself as one of our leading contemporary American composers, a man whose music was in tune with modern thought and present-day developments. Trained by Rubin Goldmark in New York and Nadia Boulanger in Paris, he was schooled in conventional theory but was also aware of twentieth century changes in musical patterns. His first important

[2] New York: Whittlesey House, 1941.

works were a Symphony for Organ and Orchestra, a Suite for Orchestra, *Music for the Theatre*, and a Piano Concerto in which he employed jazz elements in symphonic texture. At that time he felt that jazz was something the serious composer could use to advantage, but, as he explains in his book, he found that in the concerto he had done all he could with the idiom, considering its limited emotional scope. "True," he wrote,[3] "it was an easy way to be American in musical terms, but all American music could not possibly be confined to two dominant jazz moods: the 'blues' and the snappy number."

In line with the neo-classic movement as well as towards a music that is practical and workaday, Copland has aimed at a simpler music, works that are "more spare in sonority, more lean in texture." Striving for an "imposed simplicity," he has composed his highly popular *El Salón México*, a musical picture of a Mexican dance hall, based on Mexican tunes; an opera for high-school children to perform: *The Second Hurricane;* orchestral works for radio performance, a ballet, *Billy the Kid*, composed for the Ballet Caravan, using cowboy songs; and several scores for sound pictures: *The City, Of Mice and Men,* and *Our Town.*

[3] *Ibid.*

Another American who aims at simplification and who shuns the grand manner is Virgil Thomson, born in Kansas City in 1896, educated at Harvard and in Paris, and a resident of the French capital from 1925 to 1932. A few years ago he succeeded the late Lawrence Gilman as music critic of the New York *Herald Tribune*.

Thomson first came into prominence when his setting of Gertrude Stein's *Four Saints in Three Acts* was presented in New York in 1934. Here was something that was novelty plus, and many who went to laugh and scoff came away enchanted. The libretto purposely made no sense whatever. It consisted entirely of words strung along with no apparent meaning, just because the author liked the sound of them. The musical setting, however, seemed somehow to make sense of all this nonsense. Aaron Copland has written a shrewd analysis of Thomson's score. "He gave the words," writes Copland,[4] "their true speech inflection just as if their sense meaning were continuously understandable, in its emotional intention. The trick lay in making his musical emotion entirely serious and entirely unambiguous in its purpose—practically without regard to the thing said. That is what gave the opera its amusement and charm. One must add to

[4] In *Our New Music. Op. cit.*

this the inverted shock provided by Thomson's anti-
modernism. Swinging away from whatever might jar
or confuse the ear, he wrote with a simplicity unprece-
dented among contemporary composers, often confin-
ing himself to the most rudimentary scales and harmonic progressions. There may have been a minimum
of music in *Four Saints*, but in combination with the
unique costumes and stage setting . . . , the all-Negro
cast, the melodious prose of the libretto, and the fresh
scenic action, an original theater work was created
that made all other American musical stage pieces
seem dull by comparison."

In many respects, Thomson is the American counterpart of Erik Satie, the French satirist. The similarity is more one of spirit than of the actual music each
has written, but nevertheless the attitudes of the two
composers are largely the same. Thomson is an avowed
admirer of Satie, and has claimed that Satie invented
the only twentieth century musical aesthetic in the
musical world.

Just as some composers are termed neo-classic,
Thomson might be termed neo-romantic, for while
he shuns the towering and lofty flights of the German
romanticists, he never hesitates to become sentimental,
even though he may at times have his tongue in his
cheek. For thematic material, in addition to original

melodies of his own, he employs old waltz tunes, hymn tunes, French folk songs, snatches of popular songs, ancient Gregorian chants, anything that will suit his purpose.

In his belief that music's prime function is to be entertaining, and to provide relaxation, Thomson is closely allied with the *Gebrauchsmusik* movement. In this direction he has furnished scores for motion pictures, particularly the documentary films: *The River* and *The Plow that Broke the Plains;* and has composed a highly entertaining ballet-score entitled *Filling Station.* He has also written some chamber music and a symphony, but his outstanding gift seems to be in the direction of vocal works.

9

FROM PLAIN-SONG TO SWING—A

STORY OF RHYTHMS

THUS FAR ONLY passing reference has been made to the rhythmic features of modern music, to their increasing freedom and complexity. These things have been seemingly neglected, not because they are unimportant, but rather because they are so important that they require a chapter to themselves.

Without rhythm there is no music; the entire contour of any melody is determined by the regular or irregular succession of beats in which it is played or sung. If you want an example of what rhythm can do to a series of tones, go to the piano and play the scale of C downwards, starting at the C an octave above middle C. Play it slowly and regularly, and all you have is the descending scale of C major.

Then play it in the following manner, and you have

the opening phrase of the Christmas hymn, *Joy to the World:*

Rhythm existed before melody; it was present in the universe before man came into being—in the movement of the planets and the recurrence of seasons. It is the basis of vital functions—beating of the heart, breathing, as well as of such conscious activities as walking and speech. Even the cries of animals are rhythmic.

Although melody cannot exist without some sort of rhythm, rhythm is able to stand on its own feet without melody, or even without musical tone. Drum beats are merely sound, except in cases where the drums produce a tone of definite pitch, yet to many peoples, particularly primitive races, the rhythms of a drum are completely satisfying. Primitives are often found to be interested in little more than rhythm, and their drum beats are more involved and complex than the rhythms of the most advanced music of cultivated musicians.

Since rhythm is such an important factor in all music, it is inevitable that rhythmic patterns have changed and developed as music has been adapted to the needs and demands of various eras. And just as

(173)

other elements of music have changed through the centuries to reflect the background of their time, so have rhythms interpreted and expressed the contemporary life and thought of nations and peoples. It is significant that times of stress, or war, or panic, have generally produced music with exciting rhythms. Similarly, as people have grown more sophisticated, their music has been marked by subtler, more complex, rhythms. In this, however, they have often reverted to the expression of their barbaric ancestors.

Rhythms may be generally classified in two major groups: those that are measured, or strict, and those that are free. Measured rhythms are marked by regular repetitions of accent and beat and length of phrase. The opening stanza from Gray's *Elegy* is an example of measured rhythm:

The curfew tolls the knell of parting day.
The lowing herd winds slowly o'er the lea,
The plough man homeward plods his weary way,
And leaves the world to darkness and to me.

Modern poets use freer rhythms, but in doing so they are not as modern as they seem. They are actually reverting to early practice, and if we want specimens of free rhythm we need merely turn to the pages of the King James version of the Bible:

The Lord is my shepherd; I shall not want.

He maketh me to lie down in green pastures: he leadeth me beside the still waters.

He restoreth my soul: he leadeth me in the paths of
righteousness for his name's sake.

The Puritans sang the Psalms to tunes in measured
rhythm, so they had to re-translate them to fit their
purpose. In the *Bay Psalm Book*, first printed at Cam-
bridge, Massachusetts, in 1640, the 23rd Psalm was
rendered thus:

> The Lord to mee a shepheard is,
> want therefore shall not I.
> Hee in the folds of tender-grasse,
> doth cause mee downe to lie:
> To waters calme me gently leads
> Restore my soule doth hee:
> He doth in paths of righteousness:
> for his names sake leade mee.

In mediaeval plain-song the rhythm was free, and
the repetition of beats followed the accents of the
Latin text. Consequently, plain-song is not divided
into measures, and has no regular repetition of strong
and weak beats. This freedom of accent has been pre-

served to a certain extent in the recitatives of opera and oratorio.

The conception of measured rhythm in music, and its notation in symbols, resulted from the application of prosody to music, for rhythm is to music what metre is to poetry. The chorale took the place of the Gregorian chant (plain-song), and became characteristic of the reformed church of Germany and the Lutheran movement. Luther realized that his followers did not understand the Latin texts of the Roman Church, and to encourage congregational singing he adapted folk-songs, which were regularly phrased, to metrical verses. One of the most famous of these is *Ein feste Burg:*

> A mighty fortress is our God,
> A bulwark never failing;
> Our helper He, amid the flood
> Of mortal ills prevailing.

In the chorales the phrasing is regular, and each phrase is followed by a definite pause. Bach made settings of more than four hundred chorales, and they became the foundation on which the art-music of later centuries was built. They affected the structure not only of vocal music but of instrumental music as well, and we find the themes of instrumental works, well into the nineteenth century, falling into measured rhythm and definite phrases which answered and echoed each other like the metres and rhymes of a Longfellow poem. In measured music, phrases fall into patterns of two or four measures in length, separated by pauses which correspond to the punctuation of written language.

The human ear by nature conceives rhythm in units of two or three fundamental beats. Walking and marching are based on a unit of two; while dancing has for its basis either twos (four and eight, of course, are merely multiples of two) or threes. Musical time signatures, therefore, are generally derived from such units as: $\frac{2}{4}$, $\frac{4}{4}$, $\frac{2}{2}$, or $\frac{3}{4}$, $\frac{6}{4}$, $\frac{3}{2}$, etc.

In seeking freedom from the restraints of eighteenth-century music, the romantic composers liberated their rhythms as well as their harmonies and formal structures. Many of them broke away from the phrase and period structure in their melodies, and wrote longer-breathed themes which were more flexible and pliant. Sometimes they would shift the metre from two to three within the limits of a single measure.

Modern composers have learned to extend basic units to groupings not divisible by two or three. Tschaikowsky made a start in this direction by writing the second movement of his *Pathetique* symphony in $\frac{5}{4}$ rhythm. Each measure was a unit of five, or a combination of two and three.

The pattern of five in Tschaikowsky's symphony remained unchanged throughout the entire movement, but later composers, notably Stravinsky, have indulged in rapid and constant changes of time-signature. In *Le Sacre du Printemps* the rhythmic indications often change with each measure: $\frac{4}{4}$, $\frac{3}{4}$, $\frac{4}{4}$, $\frac{2}{4}$, $\frac{3}{4}$, or even $\frac{5}{4}$, $\frac{7}{4}$, $\frac{6}{4}$, $\frac{5}{4}$.

It is not only in changing and alternating basic rhythms that music has become complex, it has also combined rhythms to produce polyrhythms, just as combining two or more keys produces polytonality. Combined rhythms are not a new device; Beethoven combined two and three in his Rondo in C major:

In this passage the right hand plays three beats while the left plays two. Chopin used a two against three figure in his A flat Étude:

In his *Fantaisie Impromptu* Chopin imposed four on three:

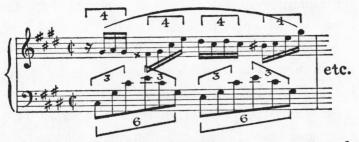

These specimens of polyrhythms are comparatively straightforward, but modern composers use combinations which are far more complex. At one point in *Le Sacre*, Stravinsky superimposes an alternating $\frac{2}{4}$ and $\frac{5}{8}$ on an underlying $\frac{3}{8}$. Charles Ives gains a novel polyrhythmic effect in *Washington's Birthday*, the opening movement of his symphony—*Holidays*. At one point the orchestra changes from a rapid allegro to a slow pace. The viola, however, is unaware of the change and continues at the rapid tempo. At another place, when the orchestra is playing at a brisk speed, the flute feels that the pace should be a trifle faster, and as a result, finishes ahead of the others. The effect is that of a village parade where the marchers have difficulty in keeping step with their fellows.

To primitive peoples such combinations of rhythms would prove child's play. It is no feat at all for an African musician to sing in one rhythm, beat his drums in another, and stamp his feet in a third. And if you want to hear really complex rhythms, listen to the album of RCA-Victor records recorded by the musicians who play for Shan-Kar, the Hindu dancer.

Nationalism in music has resulted in characteristic rhythms. The Spanish composers—de Falla, Albéniz, Granados, and others—have incorporated in their works the peculiar rhythms of Spanish folksongs and dances. The Hungarian Rhapsodies of Liszt have the rhythmic as well as the melodic irregularities of Hungarian Gypsy music. The waltzes of Johann Strauss are distinguished by the subtle accenting of the second beat in the triple waltz measure—a typically Viennese device. And all composers who have drawn on the folk-songs of the American Negro have emphasized their syncopation.

We hear a great deal about syncopation these days, and it is often looked upon as something new, developed solely for our present-day jazz and swing. Syncopation is truly an essential feature of American dance music, but as a rhythmic device it is very old, and by no means confined to any nation or any single period in the history of music. It was known to the religious composers of the Middle Ages; Bach used accenting which would seem novel trickery in the hands of a Broadway tunesmith; Beethoven was almost jazzy in the syncopation of the second movement of the *Moonlight* sonata; while Schumann wrote syncopated rhythms on almost every page of his music.

Syncopation results from shifting the rhythmic accent from the strong beats of a measure to the normally weak, or unaccented, beats. In a Sousa march, the accents fall on the normally strong beats; the tempo, and the accents, fit the swing and rhythmic cadence of marching feet: *one,* two, *three,* four; *one,* two, *three,* four; etc. The first and third beats of a group of four are the normally strong beats. Two and four are the secondary, or weak, beats.

Similarly, in measured verse, the strong beats are the ones that are normally accented:

> Lives′ of great′ men all′ remind′ us
> We′ should make′ our lives′ sublime′

If we should sing the first line of this quotation from Longfellow to the principal theme of Liszt's *Hungar-*

ian Fantasie we would have an entirely different accenting:

LIVES OF GREAT MEN ALL RE - MIND US

Thus, placing the strong accents where weak beats are expected results in syncopation. The accents may be anticipated or delayed, as long as they fall at points where they are not normally expected.

Although syncopation is found in the works of Bach, Beethoven, and Schumann, modern syncopation in the twentieth century comes from a more primitive source. It derives from the songs of the American Negro, from his spirituals and work-songs. These melodies are of vague origin, and have been influenced to a great degree by the songs of the white man which the Negro heard in this country. Nevertheless, the African heritage of the Negro, and the frenetic rhythms and syncopations of his primitive ancestors, have indisputably determined the peculiar rhythmic characteristics of American-Negro folk-songs.

Up to the latter part of the nineteenth century these rhythmic characteristics were left to the Negroes themselves; even Stephen Foster's "Ethiopian"

FROM PLAIN-SONG TO SWING

songs were not syncopated, and few of the "Negro" minstrel songs, written by white men, had any rhythmic departures from normal accenting. It was with the "coon songs" and the "ragtime" of the 1890's that Negro syncopation came into our popular music, and there began the development of a type of music, culminating in jazz and swing, which is the result of Negro music shaped by American life and surroundings and developed by white men as much as by Negroes.

Ragtime, which came into use about 1895, was comparatively straightforward. It was characterized by a so-called rhythmic snap (sometimes called the Scotch-snap because it is found also in the folk-songs of Scotland) which is produced by the false accenting we have already discussed: the accent falling on a weak rather than on a strong beat. The syncopated pattern of such early specimens as *Georgia Camp Meeting* and the *Maple Leaf Rag* was regular and consistent, and not at all involved or complex. The vogue of ragtime, however, was responsible for the later, more complicated jazz developments which have been a direct outgrowth of the early attempts at syncopation.

Nobody knows who invented jazz, nor who gave it its name. It was not familiar to the general public

(183)

until 1915, but it had probably existed among the
Negroes for some time before that. It is generally
believed that it originated in New Orleans, for a
couple of dance bands moved from that city to Chicago in 1914 and started a vogue for the new type of
dance music, a fashion which spread rapidly to other
centers of the country. Since then jazz has provided
the pattern on which almost all American dance music has been based.

Jazz music has three distinguishing features. One
is the instrumentation of its orchestra—saxophones;
muted trumpets; wailing, squealing clarinets; novel
and terrifying percussion devices. Another characteristic consists in definite melodic and harmonic traits
—"blue" notes, dissonant chords, etc. The third, and
most important, feature of jazz is found in its many
rhythms. Jazz rhythms are based on syncopation, but
a far more sophisticated and involved syncopation
than has been used in earlier music, except perhaps,
among primitive tribes in various parts of the world.
Since jazz music is primarily intended for dancing, or
some sort of bodily movement, it sets in motion an
underlying $\frac{4}{4}$ beat which continues throughout the
length of a piece. This, fundamentally, is the same
basic pattern as that of a Sousa march; but while the

Sousa march actually gives the accents you expect, jazz dodges them, and gives you an irresistible impulse to fill them in for yourself.

The obvious accents are avoided in several ways. Sometimes they are anticipated, or delayed, and on other occasions they are almost completely suppressed. The most ingenious, and complicated, method is the setting up of conflicting accents, resulting in polyrhythms. The most accepted method of using conflicting rhythms is having the bass parts beat a regular, monotonous four-four meter, while the upper parts, and the melody, employ counter rhythms and dodge the normal, expected accents.

In George Gershwin's *I Got Rhythm* the bass maintains a compound two figure, which is really four, and the melody enters on the off beat (the second half of the first beat). By using dotted quarter-notes (which are equal in duration to one and a half quarter-notes) the melody shifts its accent so that it falls with the accent of the bass only once in each phrase:

Jazz music follows two main streams, more or less distinct from each other. One comes from the folk art of Negro musicians, and the shouting and crooning of the untrained colored singer. The other branch is more commercialized and standardized: the Tin-Pan-Alley product, which comes primarily from the same source, but which is written out in all its instrumentation by an arranger, so that the performers need merely follow the notes in the music.

The first type of jazz allows, and demands, spontaneous improvisation by the performers. The printed notes may be in front of the players, but they are largely ignored, and each musician improvises freely on the harmonic basis of an agreed-upon tune. The result abounds in cross rhythms, highly dissonant counterpoint, and ingenious melodic development. All of this has produced a musical cult which has gathered to its ranks millions of fans and devotees, who worship what has become known as "swing" music. No further description is needed for the reader who listens to the radio and phonograph or spends his evenings at night-clubs.

If ragtime, jazz, and swing had remained solely in the province of Broadway, and the dance and entertainment field, we should not be concerned with them in this volume. They have, however, exerted such a profound effect on art music, particularly with their rhythmic patterns, that they are one of the most important factors in modern music. This may be because jazz is so thoroughly expressive and characteristic of many features of our twentieth-century life; of the restlessness, the overturning of tradition, the economic, social, and political upheavals of the last few decades. In fact, it was so much an expression of the 1920's that those years are known to us, and will probably go down in history, as the "jazz age." Added to all this is the emotional fury of the two most devastating wars that have ever been inflicted on mankind. Why shouldn't the music of such times be dislocated and out of step?

It is not only in America that serious composers have incorporated jazz ideas into their works. American dance music has always been popular abroad, particularly in Paris; so even before American symphonists had begun to experiment with native jazz, such composers as Stravinsky with his *Ragtime,* Milhaud with his *La Création du Monde,* Tansman with his *Tryptique,* Křenek with *Jonny spielt auf,* and dozens of others, were making capital of these typically American patterns. Whether or not they succeeded in producing the real thing, or only a synthetic imitation, is a matter for debate.

In America, of course, there have been dozens, if not hundreds, of composers who have dipped into the jazz grab bag for native material. John Alden Carpenter incorporated jazz patterns in his ballets, *Skyscrapers* and *Krazy Kat.* Louis Gruenberg, born in Russia in 1884 but living in America since he was two years old, made sincere attempts to overcome the rigidity of jazz in *Jazettes, The Daniel Jazz, The Creation,* and a *Jazz Suite* for orchestra. Edward Burlingame Hill (1872) made a gentlemanly bow to jazz in his *Jazz Studies* for two pianos, and we have already learned how Aaron Copland turned to jazz in his early works and then decided he had had enough of it, because its expressive possibilities were too limited.

The fact that jazz is primarily a dance vehicle, and that it is based on a regular, monotonous, four-beat foundation, is in itself a serious limitation. If the composer does away with the fixed background, he ceases to write jazz. It is quite true that jazz has ele-

(188)

ments which are unmistakably American, and indisputably twentieth-century, and there can be no doubt that the impression it has made will be a lasting one, for it has introduced elements in music which will be useful to composers for many generations. It is not so certain, however, that in its native, primal state it has proved fully satisfying and rewarding to composers of art-music.

The composers already cited have been musicians who approached the popular medium of jazz from the viewpoint of the concert hall and grand opera house. They are musicians who have been educated in the conservatories or by private teachers steeped in the traditions of so-called serious music, and they have turned to jazz in the same way that art composers for many generations have drawn upon the folk-music of the people.

There is, however, another group which has approached the matter from the opposite direction. These composers have started their careers as Tin-Pan-Alley song writers, and have graduated, if that is the word, to the regions of the concert hall. Generally they have produced a more genuine jazz product than those who started from the concert hall, but have been handicapped by lack of symphonic technique.

(189)

The best-known member of this group is the late George Gershwin (1898–1937) who started his musical career as a song plugger for a Broadway publishing firm. He soon began writing songs of his own, chiefly for musical comedies, which were so spontaneous, so gay and fresh in their unexpected twists of rhythm, melody and harmony, that their composer was soon looked upon as one of our most promising Broadway talents. In 1924 the larger Gershwin emerged and startled the music world with a symphonic work for piano and orchestra which incorporated all the instrumental, harmonic and rhythmic elements of jazz: his *Rhapsody in Blue*, played for the first time at Paul Whiteman's historic concert of symphonic jazz. From that time Gershwin played a dual role; he enjoyed a flourishing Broadway career which was extended to Hollywood, and also composed a succession of serious works which have become standard items in the symphonic repertoire: the Concerto in F, for piano and orchestra; *An American in Paris;* a Second Rhapsody; a set of Preludes for piano (which have been scored for orchestra), and the Negro folk-opera, *Porgy and Bess,* produced by the Theatre Guild in 1935, and revived for a record-breaking run on Broadway in 1942.

Whatever may be said of Gershwin, one thing is certain: he produced a genuine jazz product which was the real thing, a Broadway treatment of the Negro folk-idiom. He did not turn out the polite jazz which serious composers who adopted it consciously have been accustomed to write. Gershwin's scores are racy and native, and self-conscious only in their attempt to be something more than they really are. He had his limitations and was sometimes at a loss to cover a large canvas consistently and with coherent unity; but in everything he wrote he kept the tunefulness, the gayety and sparkle, that rendered all his works spontaneous and real.

There are others who have started on Broadway or with dance bands, as composers or arrangers. Ferde Grofé (1892–), composer of the *Grand Canyon Suite*, *Three Shades of Blue*, *Mississippi Suite* and other works, was arranger for Paul Whiteman, and it was he who orchestrated Gershwin's *Rhapsody in Blue*. Robert Russell Bennett (1894–), composer of the opera, *Maria Malibran* and of a number of symphonic pieces, is a skilled arranger of scores for musical comedies. William Grant Still (1895–), the Negro composer of an *Afro-American Symphony*, and of works which enjoy frequent performances by symphony orchestras, learned his trade by arranging and orchestrating for W. C. Handy, Paul Whiteman, and Don Voorhees.

Recognition of jazz as a genuine musical expression has accomplished two results: it has provided serious composers with an idiom, however limited, which has brought freshness and a new spirit into their work. It has also raised to the level of serious composers a number of genuinely creative musicians from the popular field who have had something original to say in a manner that is true to twentieth-century American life.

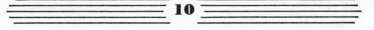

 10

TONE-CLUSTERS, QUARTER-TONES,

AND OTHER MATTERS

A NUMBER OF YEARS ago a young man named Henry
Cowell brought a letter of introduction to a manu-
facturer of player-pianos and records. It seemed that
he was a pianist-composer who had some new ideas
about piano-playing. He was invited to give a demonstration. Instead of using his fingers on the keys,
he went to work with the palms of his hands, and
finally with his entire forearms, striking whole blocks
of keys at once.

The astonished merchants were aware that Cowell
had already made something of a stir in the music
world, and that he was being taken seriously in some
quarters. They decided it might be a good idea to
have him make a recording.

Several months later Cowell realized that he had

not heard the record of his own playing, so he dropped in at the nearest store where this particular brand of records was sold. Without telling who he was, he asked to hear his piece. The clerk found it on the shelves, and inserted it in one of the pianos near the door. As the piano started to play, all the keys on the left side of the keyboard went down. In the next instant those on the right side went down. The clerk rushed to the piano. "Maybe this one is working," he said, as he took the roll out of the first piano and put it in another. The same performance was repeated, and the clerk began to perspire. "Our service man checks these pianos early in the morning," he said; "I guess he was out late last night." Being something of a wag, Cowell let the panicky clerk try a third piano, and then enlightened him.

Since then Henry Cowell has become one of the leaders of American modernists in the experimental field, and has been regarded in some quarters as the inventor of the so-called tone-clusters, or the striking, or sounding, of whole blocks, or groups, of tones simultaneously. He is not the first to employ tone-clusters; Leo Ornstein used them a quarter-century ago, and Charles Ives has written chords that must be played with a board or a ruler. Cowell, however, has gone about their development more scientifically than his predecessors, and has devised a logical basis and explanation for their use.

When Ornstein introduced them, he called them "note-clusters." At that time he was the leading radical among American composers. Some conservative critics felt that he was going in for the bizarre and startling merely because his early, conventional compositions had failed to attract much attention. To correct this state of affairs, they said, he shocked his audiences with such works as his *Wild Men's Dance,* in which he flung notes together on paper so closely that engravers had to invent new stems at crazy angles to show what notes should be struck together.

Ornstein was born in Russia in 1895 and has lived in America since 1907. He made his debut as a concert pianist in 1911, and was recognized as a musician of superior gifts. As a composer, he first produced some pieces which were altogether in traditional style, and were for the most part innocuous and undistinguished. Then, suddenly, he burst forth as a revolutionary who had thrown aside all pretense of convention. The change is described by Frederick H. Martens: [1]

[1] *Leo Ornstein, The Man—His Ideas—His Work.* New York: Breitkopf & Haertel, 1918.

". . . He found himself, after he had written much music in the major-minor system, employing traditional forms, at a serious loss to express in music those deeper and more intimate emotions and reactions within him which clamored for utterance. And then, after unhappy weeks of hopelessness and disorientation, of groping and experiment, it came to him with overwhelming suddenness—that he had discovered the alphabet of a new tongue, a tonal language which enabled him to give his inspiration the freest rein in sound expression."

Later, the author quotes Ornstein's explanation of his method of playing: "Quite often, in playing my own pieces, I use the palm of my hand. But I use it merely as a matter of convenience, since in many cases it would be physically out of the question for me to play the chord in any other way."

These sentences were written in 1918, when some of Arnold Schoenberg's new pieces were becoming known, but before the prophet of atonality had brought his system to its final completion in formulae and rules. Even at that early date, however, Schoenberg was recognized as a scientist as well as musician, and in comparing Ornstein to Schoenberg, Martens emphasized the fact that where Schoenberg was mathematical, Ornstein was guided principally by his emotions. "All that I am attempting to do," he quotes Ornstein as saying, "is to express myself as honestly and convincingly as I can in the present"; and again: "Ornstein invariably writes as he feels. . . ."

In one paragraph, the author makes a direct comparison between Schoenberg and Ornstein: [2]

"*The Wild Men's Dance, À la Chinoise*, and the *Dwarf Suite* . . . are the reflection of a logic of emotion—if one may so call it—rather than of mathematical design. Here we have the direct antithesis of Schoenberg, between whom and Ornstein it is possible to draw some analogies—Ornstein's harmonies are the natural and unalloyed result of his unfettered creative impulse, innocent of any preconceived theory; Schoenberg, on the other hand, works in accord with an abstruse and mysterious musical calculus known only to himself. For Ornstein there exist no actual chords or discords. His chord combinations are not the conscious reflexion of a definite theoretic basis, but the outcome of the impulse for a richer, fuller tonal coloring, one which extends the possibilities of pure harmony far beyond the limits of the diatonic system."

[2] *Ibid.*, pp. 41–2.

Reflections on Ornstein's sincerity were probably unjust; whatever the merits of his music, and it may be worth noting that his pieces are not much played nowadays, he no doubt was making an honest attempt to express what he wanted to say in a way that was direct and forceful. He was a youngster who knew the rules, but who decided to throw them out of the window and write to please himself.

He did attempt a partial explanation of his note-clusters. They represented, he claimed, a "perfectly logical anticipation of overtones." This anticipation of overtones, by actual playing, enabled him to secure a certain depth of tone and an effect of "clouded sonority" which it was impossible to realize in any other way.[3] There is no further explanation of the relation between Ornstein's note-clusters and overtones, but it is interesting to learn that the scientific and mathematical Henry Cowell bases his elaborate system of tone-clusters on overtones, and arrives at somewhat the same effect, though more elaborately, through use of acoustic principles and calculation of sound vibrations.

Cowell was born in California in 1897. He was largely self-educated, and having an acquisitive mind and a keen intellect, he made a thorough job of teaching himself. When he made the acquaintance of an

[3] *Ibid.*, p. 45.

old upright piano, he tried all sorts of experiments upon it. He struck the keys, and he plucked the strings. When he turned himself loose on a grand piano, he studied the sounding board, and learned where it vibrated the most.

Delighted with the startling results he achieved from haphazard experiment, Cowell set out to justify his conclusions by becoming a scientist and making himself an authority on acoustics. In a chapter on Cowell in *American Composers on American Music* [4] Nicolas Slonimsky writes:

"It is rare to find a crusader in a big cause whose intellect is as strong as his battle-ax. Not all crusaders are more interested in their cause than themselves. Few are creators of original work in a field of art. Henry Cowell is the exceptional type who possesses all of these qualities. In Pushkin's fantastic tale of Mozart and Salieri, there are these amazing lines:

And I dissected music as a corpse,
By algebra I tested harmony of sounds, . . .

This scientific procedure Henry Cowell unashamedly resumes. If there is one rule in his creative art, it consists in taking nothing for granted. Harmony, rhythm, tone-color—Henry Cowell submits them to

[4] Stanford University Press, 1933.

a test as though they were mere human beliefs, not laws."

In 1919 Cowell gathered his theories and ideas into a book, *New Musical Resources,* which was published in revised form eleven years later, in 1930. In the section on "Tone Combinations" he explains the underlying principle of his tone-clusters. Showing how each musical tone, in its vibrations, produces overtones which follow a definite harmonic pattern, he then explains that each of the overtones produces its own sub-overtones. Thus, when the tone of C produces its primary overtones of G and E, the overtone G produces its sub-overtones of D and B; and overtone E its sub-overtones of B and G sharp. When the overtones of the original C are extended further to the higher harmonics, the multiplication continues, and includes every tone of the scale. The ear, according to Cowell's theory, hears these overtones when the tone of C is sounded alone, therefore the composer is merely following scientific laws when he has them sounded simultaneously. This theory obviously ignores the fact that when a single tone is sounded, the overtones are subsidiary in sound volume to the principal tone.

Another theory of tone-clusters results from Cowell's method of constructing chords. Just as traditional harmony builds chords on intervals of the third, and the atonalists on fourths, Cowell suggests that they be built in seconds, or by the tones that are nearest to each other in the scale. This, of course, produces tone-clusters.

Cowell has also experimented widely and thoroughly in rhythms, particularly in polyrhythms which are humanly impossible for a single player, or even groups of players, to perform. These rhythms have been devised according to the rate of vibration of the pitch of each tone. For the performance of these multiple and polyrhythms, mechanical instruments may be used—player pianos, or the Rhythmicon, an instrument Cowell developed in collaboration with Professor Leon Theremin, inventor of the ether-wave instrument which bears his name.

As a composer, Cowell writes in two different styles; one embodies the scientific approach, and the other shows a Celtic love for the weird, the colorful, the whimsical, and even the sentimental. In addition to his own work, he has been a friend to all modern composers and an effective crusader for their works. He has organized concerts of new music, and has founded a quarterly periodical, *New Music,* for the publication of modern scores.

Some composers have felt that with the introduction of atonality the possibilities of the present musical scale are exhausted, and that music can go no further toward new tonal combinations unless further tones are added. This, they say, is possible only by dividing the half-tone into smaller intervals. Thus, the term quarter-tone has been introduced into the music vocabulary to indicate the division of the half-tone into two quarter-tones, so that the octave will consist of twenty-four, instead of twelve, tones. Experiments have also been made with still smaller intervals: the third-tone, sixth-tone, eighth-tone; and even the sixteenth-tone.

Orientals have long used these smaller intervals. That is why much of their music sounds out of tune to Western ears. Until recently it was generally assumed that since Oriental ears were untrained musically, according to Western standards, the Hindus and Arabs were unable to sing in tune. Scientific study, however, has shown that these people invariably sing their music in the same manner, with the same intervals, during constant repetition. They actually use these intervals intentionally.

Among cultivated musicians, Ferruccio Busoni (1866–1924) was a pioneer in using smaller intervals.

Busoni was an Italian composer, pianist, and teacher, and in his book, *A New Esthetic of Music,* he showed how the possibilities of the traditional scale could be exhausted. Then he explained how one hundred and thirteen different scales could be produced by the use of third-tones, which result from dividing the whole tone into three steps instead of the accustomed two. He later recommended a sixth-tone system.

Busoni was considerably ahead of his time, and his ideas were mostly dreams for the future: of a piano which would be built for tuning in smaller intervals, and of works written in his "triparte" scale. Later composers have been able to hear their ideas carried out, and to write quarter-tone music which has been played, either on stringed instruments which can produce tones at any pitch the player wishes, violin, viola, 'cello, etc., or on especially constructed keyboard and wind instruments.

Alois Hába, a Czecho-Slovakian composer born in 1893, is among the most prominent of those who have written quarter-tone music. The bulk of his early works were in the traditional half-tone system, but he has written many quarter-tone compositions: two operas—*The Mother* (1929) and *The Unemployed* (1932); three string quartets; violin and 'cello solo pieces; works for orchestra; and five suites and ten fantasies for piano. More recently he has been composing in sixth- and twelfth-tones.

Notation of quarter-tone music presents problems. Some composers indicate smaller intervals by notes of different shapes, and others draw lines through the stems of the notes, the direction of the lines showing whether the quarter-tones lie above or below the half-tones which the notes indicate in traditional music notation. Notation of still smaller intervals becomes even more complicated.

Julián Carillo, a Mexican composer, born in 1875, has spent more than forty years in research and experiment among small intervals of the scale. He has invented special instruments which can play these intervals: a quarter-tone guitar, an eighth-tone *octarina*, a French horn which plays sixteenth-tones, and a sixteenth-tone *arpacitera*. Some of Carillo's works have been recorded for the phonograph, notably his *Preludio a Cristobal Colon*,[5] played in quarter-, eighth-, and sixteenth-tones, by "The Thirteenth Sound Ensemble of Havana," an organization which uses Carillo's new instruments. The sounds produced by this record are indeed novel and strange to unaccustomed ears. The opening notes of the guitar sound very much

[5] Columbia Records, 7357-M.

as though the performer was tuning his instrument before actually playing, and later passages closely resemble an air-raid siren. When a human voice enters the scene, one wonders how the singer is able to maintain the pitch. The whole affair reminds one of the story of the Chinaman who was taken to his first symphony concert. He arrived early, before the orchestra had settled itself on the stage and gone through the tuning-up process. When asked afterwards how he enjoyed the concert, he said that he liked best the part that came before the works on the printed program.

Nevertheless, there is a strange beauty in this Carillo *Preludio*. It is weird and somewhat disconcerting, but it cannot by any means be dismissed as nonsense.

Among those who have developed systems of notation for small intervals are Nicholas Oboukhov and the Russian refugee, Nicholas Wischnegradsky. Wischnegradsky has written quarter-tone music for strings, and for a quarter-tone piano which was made for him in Germany.

In America, one of the leading exponents of quarter-tone music is Hans Barth, a pianist who was born in Germany in 1897, and was brought to this country as a child. Barth has had constructed a piano with two keyboards and two sets of strings. Each set of strings is tuned a quarter-tone apart from the other. In addition to a number of other works, he has composed a quarter-tone Concerto for Piano and Strings, performed by the Philadelphia Orchestra under Leopold Stokowski in 1930.

The Polish-American musicologist, Joseph Yasser (1893–), believes that where our present tonal system consists of twelve tones, seven of them primary and five auxiliary, the tonal system of the future should divide the octave into nineteen equal intervals with twelve primary and seven auxiliary tones. This, of course, would require an entirely new division of the octave, and could not utilize the present twelve-tone system by subdivision of the whole- or half-tone. Another musicologist, Arthur Fickenscher (1871–) of the University of Virginia, has divided the octave into sixty intervals, and has invented an instrument, the "Polytone," to further his research.

Edgar Varèse, born in Paris in 1885, and living in America since the first World War, has not gone in for tone-clusters or quarter-tones as such, but since he uses percussion instruments extensively, sometimes eliminating all instruments which produce a definite pitch, he may properly be discussed in this chapter.

Once when Varèse was asked if he should be classified with this or that group of modernists, he replied: "Right wing, liberal, left wing, applied to any Art, what nonsense! I try to fly on my own wings."

In this he has certainly succeeded; no one will deny his originality. Lawrence Gilman once wrote: [6] "The music of Edgar Varèse is the pure milk of Modernism. Mr. Varèse makes no such disgraceful compromise with euphony as do his more conventional brethren. Hearing Schoenberg's *Five Pieces* for orchestra, you will remember that Wagner once lived; hearing Casella's *Alta Notte* you will remember that Schoenberg still lives. Hearing Varèse's *Hyperprism* you remember only Varèse."

Hyperprism, written in the 1920's, employs a chamber orchestra and a veritable host of the percussion instruments of which Varèse is so fond, in this case with an added set of sleigh-bells and a siren. Another piece, *Ionisation* (1931) is scored for two groups of percussion instruments, played by sixteen players, or rather, instruments which the composer designates as "percussion, friction, and sibilation," excluding any which have definite pitch.

Criticism of Varèse has run all the way from his being called the greatest of modern American composers, and the author of sincere music of "remote

[6] New York *Herald Tribune*, December 17, 1924.

and alien beauty," to condemnation of his works as "strong, arrogant, infinitely repellent." For himself, he denies the charge of seeking primarily for originality, he claims that he is not interested in novelty or virtuosity, but only in expressiveness. Yet, when he stated that he is awaiting the development of electrical instruments which will give expression to certain musical concepts beyond the range of existing media, he admitted that he refuses to submit himself only to sounds that have already been heard.

⌒〰⌒

The reader who has followed these pages has gained, we hope, some idea of the directions modern music has been following, and become familiar with a few of the fundamental differences between yesterday's music and that of today. He is now able to listen to atonal or polytonal music with a different set of standards and criteria from those he applies to the older masters. No one can expect the same kind of pleasure from Stravinsky's *Rite of Spring* that he receives from *The Swan* of Saint-Saëns; nor, for that matter, will he derive from Benny Goodman the same experience he had from listening to the dance orchestra of the last generation playing the *Blue Danube*.

The important fact is that modern music is *our*

music, written in our time. Our age is not the age of our grandfathers, nor even of our fathers. Our music, therefore, reflects what has been going on about us, and if it fails to picture these things, it is dishonest and false.

The listener who approaches modern music must put aside the idea that it will give him the same emotional reactions he gets from Beethoven or Mendelssohn. From them he gets a response which is almost a direct reflex. His immediate reaction to modern music will be entirely different, and he will have to condition his natural reflex with an intellectual control which will enable him to look upon new music objectively, and decide what it is all about.

Consequently, a new yardstick must be adopted if the listener is to form a well-reasoned opinion of his own about the new music he hears. He must shelve for the moment the question of whether or not he likes it. He probably won't, but that does not mean that he will not come to like some of this music when he has heard it a few times.

First, he should decide whether the music is a true expression of the present day, or of the era in which it was written. It may, of course, represent any one, or several, of the multiple phases of our existence— idealism, unrest, optimism or pessimism, the will to freedom, hope, or despair. It may be music which comes from a free people, or from one that is in bondage.

If the listener becomes sufficiently acquainted with the architectural structure of music, so that he can follow instinctively the relation of various sections of a composition to the whole, then he can judge for himself whether the new work is coherent and unified, and whether or not the composer arrives at the place he set out for.

The listener can decide, too, whether the dissonances he hears serve an artistic purpose. They will probably disturb him, that is inevitable at first, but he can at least judge whether or not they are essential to the composer's purpose, and whether they are effective in achieving that end. When he hears polytonal music, and knows that it is employing combined keys, or tonalities, he can decide whether such a combination adds new colors to the composer's pallette.

There will, of course, be an emotional reaction; maybe it will be violent. The listener must then judge whether his emotions are those the composer intended him to have. The new piece may fill him with anger, it may give him a sense of unrest or excitement, it may even soothe him, or it may exalt him. If it does anything except bore him, it has accomplished some purpose, and time is needed to decide whether that purpose is worth while.

It is wiser, however, to consider listening to new music an intellectual sport at first, for as such it can easily prove fascinating. Then, when the strange idioms are no longer strange, the emotional pleasure will come automatically. Tomorrow you will come to like the best of today's modern music.

It is perhaps idle to speculate on what the music of the future will be; whether it will go on developing new dissonances to confuse us: quarter-tones and new scales which will always keep us a few steps behind the composers, and cause writers to keep on writing books on modern music. It is safe to prophesy, however, that the future condition of the human race will determine the course our music will take. If there is continued strife and unrest, music will be clashing and restless; if there is peace, it will reflect our composure as well as our post-war problems.

It is well to consider the qualities that have marked the enduring music of the past. Some of the most revolutionary works have lived the longest, but it is not likely that their revolutionary character, in itself, has been responsible for their immortality. Carl Engel

(211)

had some shrewd words to say on this subject a number of years ago, in an article from which we have already quoted: [7]

"The general hysteria of the moment finds vent in grotesqueness, exaggeration and caricature. The tonal material, made subservient to these ends, has yielded astonishing off-shoots and unsuspected fascinations. Yet here, too, surfeit will be reached sooner or later and change will be inevitable. Perhaps even, after the welter of mock-passion, a benign fate may lead mankind to re-discover serenity. For the noblest music, among admittedly great music, is that which fills the hearer with a serene earnestness and calm."

There are definite signs that a reaction against the extreme is taking place. Certainly Arnold Schoenberg has passed from the outermost realms of atonality to music which is far less bizarre, and which sounds rather conventional in comparison with his experimental works. Stravinsky, too, has softened his sharpest and hardest edges. One thing is certain, it is no longer fashionable to shock audiences just for the sake of startling them out of their complacency. Nobody

[7] "Harking Back and Looking Forward," *Musical Quarterly*, January, 1928.

is very smug these days, so it isn't as much fun to upset people.

It is probably true that the height of the early twentieth-century experimentation has been passed. A vast amount of new styles and methods have been tried, and some of them have been kept and some discarded. We have probably come to the time when composers have sampled enough of the new systems to have found what has served their purpose, and what is useless to them. They have absorbed into their own techniques various of the new devices and have become accustomed to using them. And since they are no longer new toys, they have learned how to use them with discretion and taste. And as pure experimentation passes, true creativeness steps in, and art takes the place of science.

All of this may well usher in a new era of music, and bring to the middle of the twentieth century a golden age from which a new music will come, built upon the best of former centuries. It will make use of new materials, tested to survive, which enable composers to write of the age in which they are living.

APPENDIX I

SELECTED LIST OF BOOKS ON MODERN MUSIC

Bauer, Marion. *Twentieth Century Music*. G. P. Putnam's Sons, 1933.

Chávez, Carlos. *Toward a New Music: Music and Electricity*. (Translated from the Spanish by Herbert Weinstock). W. W. Norton, 1937.

Copland, Aaron. *Our New Music*. Whittlesey House, 1941.

Cowell, Henry. *New Musical Resources*. Alfred A. Knopf, 1930.

Cowell, Henry, editor. *American Composers on American Music: A Symposium*. Stanford University Press, 1933.

Ewen, David. *Twentieth Century Composers*. Thomas Y. Crowell, 1937.

Gray, Cecil. *A Survey of Contemporary Music*. Oxford University Press, 1927.

Hába, Alois. *Neue Harmonielehre* (Quarter-, third-, sixth- and twelfth-tone systems). Leipzig, Kistner & Siegel, 1927.

Helmholtz, Hermann von. *Sensations of Tone.* Longmans, Green, 1912.

Heyman, Katharine Ruth. *The Relation of Ultra-Modern to Archaic Music.* Small, Maynard, 1921.

Hobson, Wilder. *American Jazz Music.* W. W. Norton, 1939.

Howard, John Tasker. *Our Contemporary Composers: American Music in the Twentieth Century.* Thomas Y. Crowell, 1941.

Křenek, Ernst. *Music Here and Now.* W. W. Norton, 1939.

Lenornaud, René. *Study of Modern Harmony.* Boston Music Co., 1915.

Miller, Dayton C. *Science of Musical Sounds.* Macmillan, 1916.

Miller, Horace Alden. *New Harmonic Devices.* Oliver Ditson, 1930.

Panassié, Hugues. *Hot Jazz: The Guide to Swing Music.* M. Witmark, 1936.

Pannain, Guido. *Modern Composers.* E. P. Dutton, 1933.

Redfield, John. *Music: a Science and an Art.* Alfred A. Knopf, 1928.

Sargeant, Winthrop. *Jazz, Hot and Hybrid.* Arrow Editions, 1938.

Slonimsky, Nicolas. *Music Since 1900* (A Chronological Record of Important Events). W. W. Norton, 1937.

Stravinsky, Igor. *About My Life* (An Autobiography). Simon & Schuster, 1936.

APPENDIX II

SELECTED LIST OF RECORDINGS

OF MODERN MUSIC

ABBREVIATIONS: C – Columbia   D – Decca   R – Royale
V – RCA-Victor   NMR – New Music Recordings
S – Schirmer

ALBÉNIZ, ISAAC
Córdoba (piano): Jose Iturbi. V.
Malagueñas (piano): George Copeland. V.
Tango in D (piano): George Copeland. V.

BARTÓK, BÉLA
Quartet for Strings, No. 1, in A minor: Pro Arte Quartet. V.
Quartet for Strings, No. 2, in A minor: Budapest Quartet. V.
Roumanian Folk Dances (violin and piano): Bartók and Joseph Szigeti. C.

BERG, ALBAN
Violin Concerto: Louis Krasner and Cleveland Orchestra. C.

BENNETT, ROBERT RUSSELL
Hexapoda (violin and piano): Louis Kaufman and Bennett. C.

BLISS, ARTHUR
Music for Strings: BBC Orchestra. V.

BLOCH, ERNEST
Concerto Grosso: Curtis Chamber Music Ensemble. V.
Quintet for Strings and Piano: Alfredo Casella and Pro Arte Quartet. V.
Schelomo ('cello and orchestra): Emanuel Feuermann and Philadelphia Orchestra. V.
Suite for Viola and Piano: William Primrose and Fritz Kitzinger. V.

CARPENTER, JOHN ALDEN
Adventures in a Perambulator: Minneapolis Symphony Orchestra. V.
Skyscrapers: Victor Symphony Orchestra. V.

CARILLO, JULIÁN
Preludio a Cristobal Colon: Thirteenth Sound Ensemble of Havana. C.

CASELLA, ALFREDO
La Giara: Milan Symphony Orchestra. C.

COPLAND, AARON
Music for the Theatre: Boston Symphony Orchestra. V.
El Salón México: Eastman-Rochester Orchestra. V.
Variations for Piano: Copland. C.

COWELL, HENRY
Movement for String Quartet: Dorian String Quartet. C.
Suite for Wood Winds; Barrère Ensemble. NMR.

DEBUSSY, CLAUDE
L'Après-midi d'un faune: London Philharmonic. C.

DEBUSSY, CLAUDE (*continued*)

Ibéria: New York Philharmonic-Symphony. V.

Nocturnes: Philadelphia Orchestra. V.

Préludes, Book I (piano): Walter Gieseking. C.

Préludes, Book II (piano): Walter Gieseking. C.

Quartet for Strings: Budapest Quartet. C.

Suite Bergamasque (piano): Walter Gieseking. C.

DELIUS, FREDERICK

Brigg Fair: Orchestra cond. by Sir Thomas Beecham. C.

On Hearing the First Cuckoo in Spring: Royal Philharmonic. C.

Walk to the Paradise Garden, from Village Romeo and Juliet: Royal Philharmonic. C.

FALLA, MANUEL DE

Concerto for Harpsichord, Flute, Oboe, Clarinet, Violin, and 'Cello: Ensemble with composer at the harpsichord. C.

Three Dances from The Three-Cornered Hat: Boston "Pops" Orchestra. C.

GERSHWIN, GEORGE

An American in Paris: Paul Whiteman's Orchestra. D.

Concerto for Piano and Orchestra: Jesús Maria Sanromá with Boston "Pops" Orchestra. V.

Porgy and Bess, Separate selections by various artists: C, D, V.

Three Preludes (piano): Gershwin. C.

Rhapsody in Blue: Gershwin with Paul Whiteman's Orchestra. V.

GLINKA, MIKHAIL

Russlan and Ludmilla, Overture: Boston "Pops" Orchestra. V.

GRIFFES, CHARLES T.

  The Pleasure Dome of Kubla Khan: Minneapolis
    Symphony Orchestra. V.

  The White Peacock (piano): Olga Samaroff-Stokow-
    ski. V. (orchestra): Eastman-Rochester Orches-
    tra. V.

HANSON, HOWARD

  Symphony No. 2, "Romantic": Eastman-Rochester
    Orchestra. V.

HARRIS, ROY

  Sonata (piano): Johana Harris. V.

  Symphony "1933": Boston Symphony Orchestra. C.

  Symphony No. 3: Boston Symphony Orchestra. V.

  Symphony for Voices: Westminster Choir. V.

  When Johnny Comes Marching Home, Overture:
    Minneapolis Symphony Orchestra. V.

HINDEMITH, PAUL

  Kleine Kammermusik, Opus 24, No. 2: Los Angeles
    Wind Quintet. C.

  Quartet for Strings No. 3, Opus 22: Coolidge Quar-
    tet. V.

  Sonata for Viola alone: Paul Hindemith. C.

  Trauermusik (viola and orchestra): Hindemith with
    string orchestra. V.

HONEGGER, ARTHUR

  Concertino (piano and orchestra): Eunice Norton
    and Minneapolis Symphony Orchestra. V.

  Pacific 231: Grand Symphony Orchestra. D.

  Pastorale d'Été. Grand Symphony Orchestra, cond.
    by the composer. D.

  Rugby: Grand Symphony Orchestra. D.

(220)

IVES, CHARLES
Barn Dance: Pan-American Orchestra. NMR.
67th Psalm: Madrigal Singers. C.

KODÁLY, ZOLTÁN
Háry János Suite: Minneapolis Symphony Orchestra.
V.

KŘENEK, ERNEST
Jonny spielt auf, Selections: Ludwig Hofmann. D.
Medley: Dajos Béla Orchestra. D.
Eleven Pieces, Opus 83 (piano): Ernst Křenek. C.

LOEFFLER, CHARLES MARTIN
Music for Four Stringed Instruments: Coolidge
Quartet. V.
Quintet for Strings: Kay Rickert with Gordon String
Quartet. S.

MILHAUD, DARIUS
Concerto for Piano and Orchestra: Marguerite Long
with Orchestre Nationale. C.
La Création du monde (ballet music): Orchestra
cond. by composer. C.
Opéras-Minutes: Conducted by the composer. C.

MOSSOLOV, ALEXANDER
Soviet Iron Foundry: Boston "Pops" Orchestra. V.

MOUSSORGSKY, MODESTE
Boris Godounov, (opera) Symphonic Synthesis:
Philadelphia Orchestra. V.
Night on a Bare Mountain: Concerts Colonne Or-
chestra. C.
Pictures at an Exposition (piano) Alfred Mirovitch.
R. (orchestra): Boston Symphony Orchestra. V.

PISTON, WALTER

Festival Song: Harvard Glee Club. V.

The Incredible Flutist: Boston "Pops" Orchestra. V.

Quartet No. 1: Dorian String Quartet. C.

Sonata for Violin and Piano: Louis Krasner and Walter Piston. C.

PROKOFIEFF, SERGE

Classical Symphony: Minneapolis Symphony Orchestra. C.

Concerto, No. 3, for Piano and Orchestra: Prokofieff and London Symphony Orchestra. V.

Concerto No. 1, for Violin and Orchestra: Joseph Szigeti and London Philharmonic. C.

Concerto No. 2, for Violin and Orchestra: Jascha Heifetz and Boston Symphony Orchestra. V.

The Love for Three Oranges, Six Sections: Orchestra of the Concerts Poulet. D.

Pas d'Acier (ballet): London Symphony Orchestra. V.

Peter and the Wolf: Frank Luther, narrator, with Decca Symphony Orchestra. D.

RAVEL, MAURICE

Bolero: Grand Orchestre Symphonique de Paris. V.

Daphnis et Chloe, Suite No. 1: Paris Conservatory Orchestra. V.

Daphnis et Chloe, Suite No. 2: Boston Symphony Orchestra. V.

Pavane pour une Infante défunte: Kostelanetz Orchestra. C.

Sonatine (piano): Alfred Cortot.

Valses nobles et sentimentales: Paris Conservatory Orchestra. V.

RESPIGHI, OTTORINO
Fountains of Rome: New York Philharmonic-Symphony Orchestra. V.
Pines of Rome. Paris Conservatory Orchestra. V.

SATIE, ERIK
Gnossienne, No. 1 (piano): George Copeland. V.
Gymnopédie, No. 1: Boston Symphony Orchestra. V.
Gymnopédie, No. 2: Philadelphia Orchestra. V.

SCHOENBERG, ARNOLD
Gurre-Lieder: Philadelphia Orchestra. V.
Six Little Piano Pieces: Jesús Maria Sanromá. V.
Pierrot Lunaire: Ensemble cond. by composer. C.
Verklaerte Nacht: Minneapolis Symphony Orchestra. V.

SCRIABIN, ALEXANDER
Poème d'Extase; Prometheus: Philadelphia Orchestra. V.

SHOSTAKOVITCH, DMITRI
Symphony No. 1: Cleveland Orchestra. C.
Symphony No. 5; Philadelphia Orchestra. V.

SIBELIUS, JAN
Concerto for Violin and Orchestra: Heifetz with London Philharmonic. V.
Finlandia: Cleveland Orchestra. C.
Symphony No. 1: Minneapolis Symphony Orchestra. V.
Symphony No. 2: Boston Symphony Orchestra. V.
Symphony No. 3: London Symphony Orchestra. V.
Symphony No. 4: London Philharmonic Orchestra. V.
Symphony No. 5: Boston Symphony Orchestra. V.

SIBELIUS, JAN (*continued*)

Symphony No. 6: Finnish National Symphony Orchestra. V.

Symphony No. 7: BBC Symphony Orchestra. V.

STRAUSS, RICHARD

Also sprach Zarathustra: Boston Symphony Orchestra. V.

Don Juan: Pittsburgh Symphony Orchestra. C.

Don Quixote: Philadelphia Orchestra. V.

Ein Heldenleben: Cleveland Orchestra. C.

Till Eulenspiegel: Cleveland Orchestra. C.

Tod und Verklärung: London Symphony Orchestra. V.

STRAVINSKY, IGOR

The Fire Bird: Symphony Orchestra cond. by composer. C.

Histoire du Soldat: Ensemble cond. by composer. C.

Les Noces: Singers and percussion ensemble cond. by composer. C.

Octet for Wind Instruments: Ensemble cond. by composer. C.

Petrouchka: Philadelphia Orchestra. V.

Pulcinella Suite: Chamber orchestra cond. by composer. C.

Ragtime: Ensemble cond. by composer. C.

Le Sacre du printemps: Philadelphia Orchestra. V.

VARÈSE, EDGAR

Ionisation: Percussion ensemble. C.

WILLIAMS, RALPH VAUGHAN

Fantasia on a Theme by Thomas Tallis: BBC String Choir. V.

Folk Song Suite: CBS Symphony Orchestra. C.

"London" Symphony: Queen's Hall Orchestra. D.

Symphony in F minor: BBC Orchestra. V.

INDEX